THE GHOST OF WHITE WOMAN CREEK

THE GHOST OF WHITE WOMAN CREEK

Robert Peterson

Deeds Publishing | Athens

Published by Deeds Publishing in Athens, GA
www.deedspublishing.com

Printed in The United States of America

Cover design by Mark Babcock. Text layout by Matt King.

Library of Congress Cataloging-in-Publications data is available upon request.

ISBN 978-1-947309-68-5

Books are available in quantity for promotional or premium use. For information, email info@deedspublishing.com.

First Edition, 2019

10 9 8 7 6 5 4 3 2 1

This book is dedicated to the brave pioneers that ventured westward and settled this great nation. They traveled via foot, boat, horseback, and covered wagon. They were of adventuresome and hardy stock. They endured many hardships along the way, but still they came, and somehow, against all odds, they survived and achieved their goals.

CONTENTS

ACKNOWLEDGEMENTS

I would like to thank my wife, Sandra, for putting up with all my rantings and ravings about White Woman Creek, Indians and supporting me in locating and collecting information for this book. Without her support this book would never have been written. I would also like to thank Nadine Chaney of the Greeley County Museum/Historical Society in Tribune, Kansas for her initial support and input regarding the history of White Woman Creek.

INTRODUCTION

Memories, memories, memories…

Years ago when my three sons were young and inquisitive they would ask me about my wife's and my youth's younger days. It was easy to relate to them of both our younger days since we both lived in the same small town in Kansas where everyone knew everyone and nothing escaped the eyes and ears of the locals.

As with most story tellers we often tend to exaggerate and embellish our stories somewhat and I am no exception to the rule. When telling a story to my sons when they were young and impressionable I would sometimes play the part of the person in my story. For example, I would play the part of a pirate if I was telling them about Treasure Island or I would be Scrooge or Santa Claus in some of my Christmas stories.

Recently my wife and I have become interested in finding out who our ancestors were. We joined ancestry.com and it has been an eye-opener for both of us. Initially, I suppose, we joined ancestry because our sons have no clue as to what it was like living in a small town in Kansas in the 40's and 50's and who their relatives are. A lot of their relatives they have never even met. They only know about them via pictures and by what my wife and I told them. They had no personal experience in meeting most of their relatives. In doing our ancestry searches it has made me think about my life and, consequently, I have been trying to record some of the things I did in my youth so my family could know more about their heritage.

One day I was relating to my sons how the boys back home used to play in the local creek called White Woman Creek. When they asked me why it was called that, I, as most of the people back home did, told them I didn't know for sure but that I had heard it was so named because of a white woman who had been captured and killed by Indians a long time ago. It pacified my boys but it got me to wondering about White Woman Creek and exactly why it was so named. I decided I would try to find out.

I ran into several problems in doing the research about White Woman Creek. I contacted the local museums and no one there knew for sure why or how it became known as White Woman Creek. I found out that it was originally called Poison Creek but when and why it changed its name is still a mystery to me. I tried contacting the State of Kansas Agricultural Department because I had read that it required its approval before some things could be named. Surly, I thought, there would be some kind of record as to when the creek got its name and why it was so named. I ran into a dead end. It got me to wondering why and how other things such as the names of cities were named.

It turns out that early on in our history people just started naming things and they took hold and soon they became "gospel". This word of mouth was what the city, place or thing became to be known as. Yes, cities and towns had to apply to the state to get their city charter approved. But the name of the city had already been named and agreed upon by the locals. The state did not mandate the name of cities. The locals had already named it. The state then approved or disapproved its charter after the fact. For example, in 1868, trader James R. Mead established a trading post where Wichita, Kansas is now located, and shortly afterwards surveyor Darius Munger built a house near there for use as a hotel, community center, and post office. Business opportunities attracted area hunters and traders, and a new settlement began to form. That summer, Mead and others organized the Wichita Town Company, naming the settlement after the Wichita Indian tribe. In 1870, Munger and German immigrant William "Dutch Bill" Greiffenstein filed plats laying out the city's first streets and Wichita was formally incorporated as a city on July 21, 1870.

I don't believe there was a formal recorded meeting by the people to agree upon the name of most cities. The same logic holds true with the naming of other things, such as creeks. Federal and State Highways are an exception. As far as I know the state mandates what they will be numbered and called. I know that President Eisenhower championed the formation of the Interstate Highway System. It's called the Dwight D. Eisenhower National System of Interstate and Defense Highways, commonly known as the Interstate Highway System. Construction authorized by the Federal Aid Highway Act of 1956. This act establishes the numbering system, signage and standards of the highways that criss-cross our great nation today.

As for the naming of rivers that flow throughout the country it has been rather haphazard. For example, on May 14, 1804, Lewis and Clark left St. Louis, Missouri on their famous expedition across the country to try and name a river that connected the east and west coasts per President Jefferson. They called it the

Missouri River. They discovered the three main headwaters to the Missouri and Merriweather Lewis would write in his journal on July 28th, 1805:

"Both capt. C. And myself corresponded in opinion with respect to the impropriety of calling either of these (three) streams the missouri and accordingly agreed to name them after the president of the united states and the secretaries of the treasury and state."[1]

A misconception of the naming of the river and the state of Missouri comes from Father Jacques Marquette calling the river "Pekitanoui" meaning "muddy," in May, 1673. In actuality, the river, and the state, were named after the Siouan Indian tribe whose Illinois name, Ouemessourita, means "those who have dugout canoes". Over the years, the river has been called the Big Muddy, Big River, Yellow River, numerous Indian names and a number of other names. It wasn't until Etienne de Veniard and Sieur de Bourgmont began to travel the river upstream, writing descriptions in 1713 and 1714 about it that we first see anyone use the name "Missouri" in writing, when referring to the river.[2][3]

So, as I was finding out, a lot of (most) the names of our roads (trails), rivers and cities were informally named and the names stuck. There wasn't any "formal" naming of them.

A "Question and Answer" article that was published in the Atlanta Journal Constitution illustrates this very well. It is as follows:

"Q: You sometimes answer questions about the origins of

county and city names around the state. The city of Palmetto, south of Atlanta, has an interesting name. How did it come to be known as that?

A: I'm always curious about how Georgia's counties and cities earned their names.

I've found many have been named for famous folks — war heroes, politicians or businessmen — or a person of local importance, such as a town's first postmaster, store owner or railroad exec.

And originally, Palmetto fell into this category. It was called Johnson's Store (for a postmaster) from 1833 until 1847, according to the city's website. That's when a unit of soldiers from South Carolina passed through there on its way to fight in the Mexican War.

"They said the community reminded them of their state, the Palmetto State," the website states, so the town was renamed Palmetto.

Palmetto, which is at the southern end of Fulton County was incorporated in 1853."[4]

A problem I ran into in writing this was copyrights. I found several excellent pamphlets, books, articles, stories and pictures that I wanted to use in writing this story. However, I could not use them as I don't want to be sued for copyright infringement and I didn't want to pay for the right to use them. I simply referred to them and made a notation.

It seems as though if you research something enough there will be conflicts and disagreements. Another problem I had with doing the research was the more interesting things I found I wanted to include them in this story. It was hard to write just "a little bit" about things and people that truly fascinate me. The plight of the Native American Indians, for example, could go on and on. It is, in my opinion, still occurring in America today.

Also a lot of the information I included about the Native American Indian I gleaned from Wikipedia. Unfortunately, Wikipedia is not to be cited in research papers and may be considered unacceptable, because Wikipedia is not considered a reliable source. This, fortunately, is not a research paper so I used the information from Wikipedia freely. You be the judge. I have listed some of the Wikipedia sources I used in the rear of this book after the Bibliography.

Anyway, the purpose of this little story about the White Woman Creek is mostly for my own self-satisfaction and pleasure. I just wanted to write something about the White Woman Creek and the legend of the white woman that was supposedly killed in it. There are many legends that involve ghosts in Kansas. This one is no different. One merely has to go to the Kansas Historical Society web pages to learn about some of them.[5]

I'm writing this on the assumption that the legend about Indians capturing a white woman has merit. In that regard, I wanted to find out who were the Indians involved and why they did it, if in fact they actually captured and killed a white woman. If this is what happened I wanted to ascertain who the white woman was and what happened to her. As best as I can determine it was the Cheyenne Indians that were responsible. That's why I focused on them.

I also know that a lot of what I write about regarding the history of Kansas may seem out of place but it's written merely to show that during the late 1800's times were very turbulent in Kansas. It's a wonder any of the settlers survived at all.

Most of what I've written is factual and is well documented. Some of what I've written is not. It's your job to decipher which is which.

Thank you for reading it. I hope you enjoy it.

1. INDIAN WAYS

THERE WERE MANY DIFFERENT INDIAN TRIBES THAT ROAMED and lived on the great plains of America in the late 18th and early 19th Century. The state of Kansas is named after one of them, the Kansa Indians or South Wind People. At some point in time the name Kansas took hold and the territory became known as the Kansas Territory.

It is my belief, one of these Indian Tribes, or branch thereof, was responsible for causing the small creek in Greeley County Kansas to be named White Woman Creek. I believe it was a branch of the Cheyenne Indians.

I will try to explain why.

The Cheyenne Indians were known as an indigenous people of the Great Plains, and were considered to be part of the Algonquian language-speaking people. The language is related to Arapaho but has a much more complex phonology, with vowel devoicing and tones. It is a verb-based polysynthetic language with long words, complex morphology, and fairly free word order. The Cheyenne alphabet contains only 14 letters.

Cheyenne is pronounced "Shy-ANN". It comes from the Dakota Sioux name for the Cheyennes (Sahiyenan), which may mean "relatives of the Cree" or some other people who spoke an Algonquian language related to the Cree and Cheyenne.[6]

The earliest known written historical record of the Cheyenne comes from the mid-17th century, when a group of Cheyenne visited the French Fort Crevecoeur, near present-day Chicago, Illinois. The Cheyenne at this time lived between the Mississippi River and Mille Lacs Lake in present-day Minnesota. According to tribal tradition, during the 17th century the Cheyenne had been driven out by the Ho he (Assiniboine) from the Great Lakes region to present-day Minnesota and North Dakota, where they established villages. Tradition also tells us that some of the Cheyenne reached the Missouri River in 1676. The remaining Cheyenne in the Mille Lac region of Minnesota were pushed out of Minnesota in 1765 when the Ojibwe defeated the Dakota with firearms, which pushed the Cheyenne in turn to the Minnesota River, where they were reported seen in 1766.

Today the Cheyenne Indians are made up of two Native American ethnic groups; the Northern Cheyenne, known in Cheyenne either as Notameohmesehese meaning "Northern Eaters" or simply as Ohmesehese meaning "Eaters", and the Southern Cheyenne Indians, known in Cheyenne as Heevahetaneo'o meaning "Roped People." The distinction between the two is purely geographic, although it has served to hasten the destruction of their former compact tribal organization. This separation was made permanent by the treaty of Ft Laramie in 1851.

The Northern Cheyenne, are now commonly known as "Omisis eaters," and the Southern Cheyenne, are now commonly known as Sowonia, or southerners (from the Cheyenne word Sowon, meaning south). The Northern Cheyenne was initially around the upper Platte River in Montana. It 1884 the Northern Cheyenne received their own reservation, set aside for them, by United States Presidential executive order, in the state of Montana, called the "Northern Cheyenne Reservation." The Northern Cheyenne is the larger of the two groups. The Southern Cheyenne are now permanently settled in Oklahoma.

The two groups were not always the case. Sometime early in Cheyenne history they had split into three tribes known as the Heviqsnipahis, the Sotaeo'o and the Masikota. They unified themselves to form the Tsetsehestaeste (also spelled Tsitsistas) which translates to "Like Hearted People", "those like us" or "Human Beings." The unification of the tribes was then known as the Cheyenne Nation. The Cheyenne Nation had ten principal bands and each band had four seated delegates in their annual Council of 44 chiefs. The remaining four chiefs were the principal advisers of the other delegates. Smaller bands or sub-bands had no right to send delegates to the Council of 44.

In all councils that concerned the relations of the Cheyenne with other tribes, one member of the council was appointed to argue as the proxy or "devil's advocate" for the other tribes or "alien people". This system regulated the Cheyenne military societies that developed for planning warfare, enforcing rules, and conducting ceremonies. Although they were separated geographically, they kept in touch with each other via the Council of 44 and this ensured they thought and acted as one rather than many different bands. They really valued harmony, so every council member had to agree on a decision before action could be taken. They had to have a "consensus". This council of 44 is still symbolized by a bundle of 44 "invitation sticks", kept with the sacred medicine-arrows, and formerly sent around when occasion arises to convene the assembly even today.

When originally seen by the white man they were in the northeast part of the country, mostly in Minnesota around the Great Lakes. Although none have been found it has been determined that the early Cheyenne lived in earth lodges and ate mostly fish to survive. [7] While living in the Minnesota area the Cheyenne occupied fixed villages, practiced agriculture, and made pottery and beads. It wasn't until the 1800's that the Cheyenne moved into teepees and started to become roving buffalo hunters. This was when they lost most of their arts — when they became a plains people. No longer did they have time and resources for pottery, etc. It was around that time that they also became a farming people with the women harvesting corn, squash and beans while the men mostly hunted deer and buffalo and occasionally fought with and raided other tribes.

When the Cheyenne moved into the North Dakota area, the Sioux said it was "the place where the Cheyenne plant", showing that they were still an agricultural people while living in the Dakota's. Although they still practiced, on a limited basis, agricultural planting, it was not the same to them as they had done previously. In a sacred traditional ceremony, they still tell how they "lost the corn" after leaving the eastern part of the country.

Cheyenne women were in charge of the home. Besides the farming, they did the cooking and cleaning and would build the family's house tipis (teepee). They would drag the heavy posts for the teepees with them whenever the tribe moved. It was said that a Cheyenne woman could take down her teepee in 15 minutes and be ready to move, and once at their new location could put the teepee up in less than an hour.[8]

A typical Cheyenne village had their teepees erected in a circle.[9] Each teepee had a big fire (lit by using flint) in the middle of it. They would place stones in the hot coals for warmth in winters. The teepees were put up and covered with buffalo hides. They would also build a trench around each teepee to keep the water out. Only the bare necessities such as bed rolls would go inside the teepee.

The women tanned and dressed hides for clothing, shelter, and other uses. Cheyenne women wore long deerskin dresses and they normally only had two of them. The men wore breech cloths with leather leggings. Later, Cheyenne men adopted the Plains war shirt worn by other Indians of the region. A lady's dress and warrior's shirt was fringed and often decorated with porcupine quills, shells, and elk teeth. The men wore moccasins and women wore high fringed boots. Later they adapted European costumes such as cloth dresses and vests, which they decorated with quill-work and fancy beading. Both the men and women took part in the art work. Cheyenne Indian leaders originally wore tall feather headdresses like the Blackfeet, but they soon began wearing the long war-bonnets that Plains Indians are famous for. The men wore their long hair in braids with a topknot or pompadour, and women wore their hair either loose or braided. The Cheyenne also painted their faces for special occasions. They used different patterns for war, religious ceremonies, and festive occasions like a wedding or a dance.

The women also gathered roots, berries, and other useful plants. Their lives were obviously very physically demanding. Unlike most Indian women, the Cheyenne women also took part in the buffalo hunt. They would drive the buffalo toward the warriors so they could shoot them with their long bows. A woman might occasionally become a warrior, but a Cheyenne chief was always male. As was customary with most of the prairie tribes, polygamy was permitted. A warrior could have several wives as long as he was able to provide for them. They also commonly buried their dead in trees or on scaffolds, but occasionally in caves or in the ground.

Horses were extremely important to the Cheyenne. The Spanish explorers first brought the horse to South America. Soon the Spanish traveled northward into North America in their search for gold and brought the horse. The native people learned about the horses by watching the Spaniards. It was the Spanish/Europeans that introduced the horse to North America.

An article titled "What is an American Indian Horse?" states the American Indian Horse generally has these qualities: [10]

A. Usually carries spanish barb, arabian, mustang, or foundation appaloosa blood in his veins, even if you don't know his pedigree.

B. Shows the litheness, agility, endurance and load-carrying capabilities of the bloodlines shown above. Often very flexible, intelligent, independent and able to take care of themselves—still has the "wild" streak in them that allows them to respond well to danger. However, they are friendly and courageous, easily trusted around children and pets.

C. Does not show small feet in comparison to the body

structure, overly muscled/fat body style of the "modern" breeds, overly straight legs, over defined conformation. Also does not have many of the digestive, nervous, and muscular problems associated with modern pampered breeds.

D. May be of any color, often includes the rare colors such as lilac roan, peacock spotted leopard, or overran paint. Unusual marking such as lightning marks, leg striping, line-backing, or varnish marks are much more components of breed due to the spanish barb influence. Colored appaloosas of the foundation type are common, as are the various paints, pintos, and mixtures of colors.

E. Normally a smaller, more compact animal 15 hands or less, although larger and smaller sizes are common.

F. Often has a lot of fetlock and body hair if allowed to grow out, to protect him from the elements. Hooves are hard and healthy.

G. American indian horses are highly prepared by mother nature to survive hot summers in arid deserts, frigid winters, and sloppy conditions in between: on less feed and with less care than other horses. They can be ridden long distances with fewer injuries, perform heady ranch and range work with more power, and generally provide better "horsepower" than horses much larger.

Because horses had escaped some of the early settlements or were just left behind for some reason or another it didn't take long for wild herds of horses to be on the plains. Early Indians acquired the horse mainly by finding an abandoned one, stealing some from settlers and catching some of the wild ones in the herds on the plains. Once the Cheyenne acquired the horse, their lifestyle changed almost immediately. In less than 150 years they became more migratory. It was the horse that changed the Cheyenne's style and manner of living. The horse became so important, eventually it became the center of their everyday life.

Before the horse, they lived in earthen lodges and birch-bark wigwams and were fairly stationary. They used dogs to pull their travios (a kind of drag sled) to help them carry their belongings. As their life style became more nomadic, they began to use the buffalo-hide teepees and use horses to drag their travois. With the horse, they could move faster and farther and it allowed them to follow the buffalo herds.

One of the most interesting subjects about the American Plains Indians, especially the Cheyenne Indians, is how little equipment they used to ride their horses. They made the control of their ponies seem effortless. They performed outstanding horsemanship skills with barely any equipment. The Cheyenne bridle is one of the pieces of equipment that very little is known about by modern horsemen. It consisted of a single line of rope that encircled the bottom jaw of the horse, making a loop, and then coming back to the rider. The purpose of the bridle was to stop the horse.

Guidance of the horse was communicated through the legs, knees, and feet of the rider. The materials used for making the Indian bridle were sinew material or horsehair which was braided to give them length and strength, and buckskin or hides that were cut in a coil-like pattern to achieve length. The length of the rope made would not be less than 14 feet and would sometimes be longer than 20 feet.[11] Their reason for the long lengths was simple. They were used for a tail that would either drag the ground or be tucked into the waistband. In the event the rider should fall from the horse, he would have a chance to keep his horse from getting away. There were problems with this arrangement. The horsehair bit wasn't pleasant to the horse as the buckskin rein would harden. Unfortunately, that was all the Indians had. They had to make good use of what they had, and they did.

That is why they learned to guide the horse using mostly their legs and feet to make the horse do anything they wanted. They developed good relationships with their horses. The Cheyenne became excellent horsemen and were well known for their prowess on a horse. Even General George Custer, who had little use for Indians, admired the Cheyenne for their riding skills. Every warrior had several horses, some for hunting, some for battle, and some to use as gifts. They always mounted the horse from the right side to keep their bows free.

Once the Cheyenne had horses, they began trading regularly with other tribes, settlers, and trading posts. They especially liked to trade buffalo hides for tobacco and corn. They communicated with the other tribes by using the Plains Sign Language.

The Cheyenne were mostly friendly. Their closest ally was the Arapaho with whom they shared territory. However, they also fought wars from time to time. Of course they didn't fight the way or why the Europeans did. The Cheyenne fought to prove their courage. They didn't fight over territory. That would have been senseless since they were so migratory. Although they sometimes fought to the death or to destroy something like another tribe's village, it was rare. They certainly had the equipment to do so.

They carried a strong long bow with a quiver of arrows, a war club, a knife, a hide shield, a tomahawk, a spear and, later, sometimes a long rifle or pistol or shotgun. Their warring custom, however, included counting "coup" (which meant touching an opponent in battle without harming him), stealing an enemy's weapon or horse, or forcing the other tribe's warriors to retreat. At times they fought neighboring tribes such as the Sioux, Comanches, and Kiowas. At other times these tribes were their allies. They all tended to make peace with each other shortly after the fighting.

The title of war chief could be earned by any warrior who performed enough of the specific coups required to become a war chief. Specific warrior or military societies developed. The societies played an important role in Cheyenne government. Society leaders were often in charge of organizing hunts and raids as well as ensuring proper discipline and enforcement of laws within the nation. Each of the six distinct warrior societies of the Cheyenne would take turns assuming the leadership role with the nation. The four original military societies of the Cheyenne were the Swift Fox Society, Elk Horn Scrapper or Crooked Lance Society, Shield Society, and the Bowstring Men Society. The fifth society is split between the Crazy Dog Society and the famous Dog Soldiers. The sixth society is the Contrary Warrior Society, most notable for riding backwards into battle as a sign of bravery.

The Cheyenne had a legend about dogs who turned into fierce warriors. As a result, some Cheyenne were known as Dog Soldiers/Warriors or Dog Men. They were especially brave and honorable. When one of them was defending a Cheyenne village, a Dog Soldier would stake his long belt to the ground, to show that he would not run away, but would defend his people to the death.

Like most cultures that didn't or couldn't document things via the written word, the Cheyenne people had an oral culture. Their oral history tells how the prophet, Sweet Medicine, organized their war societies, their system of legal justice, and the Council of Forty-four chiefs. The prophet, Erect Horns, gave them the Sacred Arrows and accompanying ceremonies, which they carried when they waged tribal-level war.

It was Erect Horns that convinced the tribes to abandon their earlier sedentary agricultural traditions to adopt nomadic Plains horse culture. The Cheyenne culture was one of ritual and nature. They recognized the "Wise One Above"[12] and also believed in a god beneath the ground. Their ritual dances and practices centered around the battle and the hunt, the two primary focuses of the Cheyenne after they were oppressed by foreign settlers.

Around 1811, the Cheyenne made an alliance with the Arapaho people. The alliance helped the Cheyenne expand their territory which stretched from southern Montana, through most of Wyoming, the eastern half of Colorado, far western Nebraska, and far western Kansas. As early as 1820, traders and explorers reported contact with Cheyenne at present day Denver, Colorado, and on the Arkansas River. This was when the Cheyenne split into the two main groups known as the Sowonia (Southerners) and the Omisis (Northerners). It was later that the third group, the Dog Soldiers, came into being. Again, the separation of the tribes was only a geographic one and the two divisions had regular and close contact.

When the Cheyenne were eventually forced to move to Oklahoma, the Cheyennes from the south grudgingly accepted this arrangement, but the Cheyennes from the north could not adapt to the hot weather and "broke out" to flee back to the north, led by Chiefs Dull Knife and Little Wolf.

Today, the Cheyenne still have two distinct communities: The Northern Cheyenne in Montana, which number around 7,000 and the Southern Cheyenne, who are united with their longtime allies the Arapaho into a single Nation in Oklahoma with a combined 11,000 members.

The Indian enemies of the Cheyenne included the Crow, Shoshone, Blackfeet, Flathead, Arikara, Gros Ventre, Assiniboine, Pawnee, Sioux, Ponca, Kaw, Iowa, Ho-Chuck, Omaha, Osage, Kiowa, Comanche, Ute, Plains Apache, and Wichita people. Later of course, the white man became an enemy of the Cheyenne. Many of the enemies they fought were only encountered occasionally, such as on a long-distance raid or hunt. But they happened and the Cheyenne, like other Indian tribes, had to be on the alert constantly for hostiles, be they Indian or the white man.

2. WHITE MAN'S WAYS

Part 1: White Man's Deeds

Ever since William Bradford and the Mayflower Pilgrims landed at Plymouth Rock in 1620, America has experienced a phenomenal growth in population. People from all over the world wanted to come to the new land discovered by Christopher Columbus in 1492. Although its population start was shaky at first and it has had growing pains ever since, it continued to grow. First, the people colonized the east coast and then the population movement started to spread inland.

Their reasons for wanting to come to America were as varied as the number of different types of ethnic groups. They wanted to come here to escape religious prosecution, to seek their fortune, to come as indentured servants and then stay to make a new life for themselves, and to seek adventure were just a few of the reasons.

The "white man" first met Indians on this continent as soon as the first Pilgrims arrived. First, the Pilgrims tried to convert them, then learn from them, and then eliminate them. Almost from the first encounter, whites felt Indians were an inferior race and had little or no rights. That feeling toward Indians by some whites, even today, has continued.

Yes, the early settlers worked with the Indians, shared agriculture knowledge, bartered with them, and tried to live in peace with them. However, it should be noted that the settlers were vastly outnumbered and they had to live in harmony with the Indians in order to survive. But in making deals with them, even one of our first deals with them showed our disrespect. The Dutch purchased Manhattan for a few beads and trinkets. Marth J. Lamb in History of the City of New York (1877: New York, Vol, I, p. 104) who first wrote: "He (Minuit) then called together some of the principal Indian chiefs, and offered beads, buttons, and other trinkets in exchange for their real estate. They accepted the terms with unfeigned delight, and the bargain was closed at once." The key word here is "trinkets".

From the beginning, the early settlers felt the land was theirs and not the Indians. Then the settlers (Americans) fought the Revolutionary War from 19 April 1775 to 3 Sept 1783 to win our independence from Great Britain. This was our first war with Great Britain. We wanted our freedoms, especially from taxation and for equal representation, but it is obvious we felt the land was ours and not the Indian's or Great Britain's. Ironically, the war with Britain also involved fighting Indians.

In 1781, while the Revolutionary War was going on, Andrew Jackson (who was just 14 years old) and his brother, Robert, went to help defend a meeting house against the Tories and some British Dragoons. Their older brother, Hugh, had died of heat exhaustion during a battle the previous year. The battle didn't go well with the two brothers. They had to flee. They went to their cousin's house but were soon caught by the British. A British officer drew his saber and cut Robert in the head and Andrew's left arm to the bone. They were taken prisoner. Since their father had worked himself to death prior to Andrew's birth, it was up to their mother, Elizabeth, to get the boys released from the British.

She went to where the boys were being held prisoner and obtained their release. Their shoes had been taken from them, their wounds had not been treated, and they were not being fed. They were in a bad way. In driving rain and with only two horses (Robert was delirious and rode one and Elizabeth the other) they finally made it home. Andrew walked barefoot home. Robert died two days later. Elizabeth then went to Charleston, 160 miles away, to try to get a release from prison two nephews she had helped raise that were being held prisoner there. She never returned home. She got sick and died of cholera.[13] Young Andrew would never forget the pain and suffering he had to endure because of the British!

Andrew went to live with relatives in North Carolina. Because everyone in his family was now dead, Andrew adopted America as his "new family". He became a saddler's apprentice and then clerked for a North Carolina attorney. He became a lawyer at age 21 and took an appointment as a public prosecutor in North Carolina's western district. His duties as the public prosecutor took him across the Appalachians and a few years later that district became part of the state of Tennessee (Tennessee joined the union in 1796).[14]

Then came the War of 1812. This was a 32-month war. It was from 18 June 1812 to 18 February 1815. Congress officially declared war against Great Britain in June 1812. The war was between the United States of America and the United Kingdom of Great Britain and Ireland, its North American colonies and

15

its Indian allies. The United States declared this war for several reasons. One of those reasons was British support of American Indian tribes against American expansion. The British seemed to be agitating the Indians against us.

For many years, the Five Civilized Tribes in (Cherokee, Chickasaw, Choctaw, Creek, and Seminole) were friendly with us but as more and more settlers moved into their territories, hostilities would break out, reportedly by Indians who were being agitated by British agents against us. (There you go again, the Indians didn't want us to expand but we wanted to and had to fight a war in order to survive as a country. It was the Indians loss and America's gain). Settlers were in constant fear of being attacked by Indians. There were reports of men coming home from a day in the field hunting only to find their families butchered, and of wives who had found their husbands in the field scalped. [15]

A major Shawnee uprising in 1811 escalated the fear. It was reported the British had been supplying them with weapons and promising them land if they carried out the raids against the settlers.

Another reason we declared war was because Great Britain, had already attacked the U.S. Navy's Chesapeake, killing three sailors and taking four others from the ship and impressed them into service to the crown. By the time we declared war against Britain, they had seized more than five thousand men off the decks of American ships. [16] Additionally, we had recently purchased the Louisiana Territory in 1803 from France and this vast expanse of more than eight hundred thousand square miles could not be afforded to be lost to the British. We purchased it for $15 million dollars, which equates to less than three cents an acre.

The war was dubbed as "Mr. Madison's War" by the Boston Evening Post. He was the first president to ever sign a declaration of war.[17] Others called it the Second American Revolution.

Of the many battles that were fought during the War of 1812, just a handful of them stand out. President Madison's Secretary of War, William Eustis, a Revolutionary War regimental surgeon and not a military strategist or soldier, was advised to attack the British and it's Indian allies in Canada (which was also under British rule) thereby freeing Canada from Britain and rid the British from seeking to further its threat against the U.S.

Eustis did a three-prong attack into Canada. The first was from Fort Detroit under the command of General William Hull (another veteran from the Revolutionary War that hadn't been in uniform in thirty years). This attack failed and General Hull surrendered Fort Detroit and the entire North-Western Army of the U.S to a British and Indian force half its size.

The second assault into Canada was from Niagara using New York militiamen to reinforce Ohio troops that were fighting the British. It failed miserably when the New York militiamen refused to cross the border into Canada and, consequently, 950 Ohio militiamen were taken prisoner.

The third assault was headed by a Major General Henry Dearborn (another veteran who hadn't seen combat in three decades). This assault also failed as some of the troops again refused to cross over into Canada and the remainder of them were quickly routed and retreated.

And this brings Andrew Jackson into the picture again!

The young Andrew Jackson loved drinking, playing cards, and horse racing. He also moved up in the social circle, becoming the region's first delegate to the new state's constitutional convention. He then served as Tennessee's first congressman and then became a U.S. senator. He then accepted an appointment to Tennessee's Supreme Court.

Although he was busy administering the law, Andrew found the time to marry the love of his life, Miss Rachel Donelson. This marriage also helped Andrew move up the social circle ladder as Rachel was from one of Nashville's founding families. Andrew and Rachel settled in a piece of land near Nashville. They called it "The Hermitage". (The Hermitage is now a national historical site). The Jacksons hosted many gatherings at The Hermitage. Their hospitality was well known throughout the area. Because of this, and because Andrew was politically savvy, he was elected Major General of the Tennessee militia in February 1802.[18]

The young Andrew Jackson was red headed and known for his fiery temper. So much so he fought several duels, some of which were mostly fought for matters of honor resulting in shots fired in the air and no one being injured. However, in 1806 he fought a duel and killed a man who had called him a "worthless scoundrel" and a "coward." Jackson sustained a chest wound when a lead ball broke two ribs and lodged deep in his left lung. This would never totally heal and it caused him problems later in his life.

Then on June 14, 1813, General Jackson stood by someone else's duel, resulting in a wound to the buttocks of one of the men. A Lieutenant Colonel Thomas Hart Benton blamed Jackson for not having the duel fought fairly. This infuriated Jackson and he said he would horsewhip Benton the next time he saw him. On 4 September, Lt. Col. Benton was in Nashville at the Nashville City Hotel. Jackson went to confront him and gunshots were exchanged and Jackson was shot in the left shoulder and the ball lodged in his upper arm. The Doctors wanted to remove his arm but he refused.

While the General was recovering from his wound, news came of an Indian massacre of settlers at Fort Mims. The "Red Stick Creeks" were responsible. Their chief was Chief Red Eagle, also known as William Weatherford. Weatherford was the son of a Native American Indian and a Scots trader. The Red Sticks butchered almost 300 men, women, and children. This made everyone in the country mad, especially Andrew. This was his call to action once again.

He had earlier in the year mustered up a bunch of Tennessee farmers, businessmen, and the like and tried to take them to New Orleans because that's where he felt the main threat from the British would come. The rag tag group of "Tennessee Volunteers" almost got there but he was told by the President, via the Secretary of War General John Armstrong, to take his volunteer army and go back to Tennessee. It was tough on them. They had no equipment save their own muskets and ammo. They were not in uniform and their clothes were literally falling off them. Their morale was low as they had not been paid or equipped and were going past their short enlistment times.

It was during the hard march back to Tennessee that many of them (156) became sick. Fifty-six (56) of them were so sick they could not even sit unassisted. It was during this march that Andrew Jackson started to prove himself once again. He gave his horses to the sick and walked on foot with his men. His men called him "Old Hickory" because he was as tough as an old hickory tree, despite his poor physical condition.

When the Red Stick Creek Indians massacred the people at Fort Mims, that was all Jackson needed. Jackson, now a brigadier general, gathered up his Tennessee Volunteers again. He issued orders on September 24, 1813, and 2,660 men gathered in Fayetteville, Tennessee in two weeks. Jackson then took his army and headed south toward Fort Mims to take vengeance out on the Indians. Plus, he was headed toward New Orleans again, which is where he strongly felt he and his army needed to be to defend New Orleans against the British.

This became known as the Creek War. There were friendly Creek Indians but a branch of them known as the Red Sticks (they were known as Red Sticks because they painted their tomahawks red) living in the Southeast part of the country and were fed-up with the continuing encroachments on their territory by white men and, consequently, they waged war against the U.S. Government.

In early November, Jackson's forces found a large encampment of Red Sticks near the Coosa River and, under the command of Gen. John Coffee, Jackson's forces met up with and killed 186 warriors and took 84 prisoners, all women and children. A small Indian child known as Lyncoya had lost both his parents in the battle. In a letter to his wife, Rachel, Jackson said, "Charity and Christianity says he ought to be taken care of." The Jacksons ended up adopting the child. They took him in as one of their own family and raised and educated him at the Hermitage.[19]

Just a few days later, on 7 November 1813, Jackson's scouts reported that over 1,000 Red Sticks had besieged a settlement of friendly Creek Indians near Talladega. Although Jackson was extremely sick with intestinal problems (he could barely sit up straight) and his left arm and shoulder still hurt him, he marched his forces some 25 miles to come within range of the Red Sticks. His pain was so great he would lean forward in his saddle and almost hug the horse's neck to ease his abdominal pain. Even though pain racked, he was still able to devise a plan to defeat the Indians. Once the attack began and the Indians charged, Davy Crockett wrote they were, "like a cloud of Egyptian locusts screaming like all the young devils had been turned loose, with the old devil of all at their head."[20] When the dead were counted, Chief Red Eagle (Weatherford) had lost 299 warriors to Jackson's 15 soldiers. The Red Sticks now called him "Sharp Knife."

Jackson's volunteers continued to pursue the Red Sticks and fought two more hard fought battles with them. It was during these two battles that Jackson's reputation continued to grow. And for the first time, U.S. Army regulars were put under his command in addition to the volunteers, raising the total number of troops in his command to more than 3,500.

On Mar 27, 1814, Andrew Jackson brought 2,600 American soldiers, 500 Cherokee, and 100 Lower Creek Indians to a bend in the Tallapoosa River called Horseshoe Bend. It was here they fought about 1,000 "Red Stick Creek" Indians that had been given wagon loads of supplies by the British. This was another extremely hard fought battle. Of note one of Jackson's platoon leaders was Sam Houston and during the battle he took an arrow in his upper thigh. He continued to fight and was subsequently struck with two musket balls, one in his right arm and the other his right shoulder. In the end, over 800 Red Sticks died in contrast to Jackson's forces only losing 70 men and 206 wounded. It became known as "The Battle of Horseshoe Bend."

Jackson was hailed as a hero and the Indians had to give up over 23 million acres of land, which was half of central Alabama and part of southern Georgia, to the U.S. Government.[21][22][23] Chief Red Eagle shortly afterward rode up alone into Jackson's camp and surrendered to Jackson. This battle effectively ended the Creek War.

One of the battles that stands out in the War of 1812 was the "Battle of Lake Erie" on September 10, 1813 which the American Commander, Captain Oliver Hazard Perry, fought and won and stated in a message to William Henry Harrison, "We have met the enemy and they are ours."[24]

Another significant battle was "The Battle of Fort McHenry" that also took place in September 1813. It was during this battle that inspired the American lawyer Francis Scott Key to write a poem called "Defense of Fort McHenry"[25] and that the lyrics to that poem would eventually become the lyrics to our National Anthem, "The Star-Spangled Banner".

Right after the Battle of Horseshoe Bend, Jackson's army set out for New Orleans. This was the most important battle in the War of 1812. If America lost this battle, we stood to lose the Louisiana Territory and, in all likelihood the rest of America, in time. Everything was at stake. Against all odds, Jackson's forces managed to defeat the British and their Indian allies.

After the War of 1812, the Indians and settlers were still arguing and fighting over territories. This brought about two (2) significant Indian treaties. Both took place in 1825.

The first one was the treaty with the Indians located mainly in the mid-west. It was called "The Atkinson & O'Fallon Trade and Intercourse Treaty of 1825." It was the first major treaty with tribes in that region. In the summer of 1825, a group under the control of Indian Agent Benjamin O'Fallon and General Henry Atkinson traveled up the Missouri to the Yellowstone with nine keelboats and a large military escort of 476 soldiers. Treaties were made with the Titon, Yankton, Dakota, Cheyenne, Mandan, Hidfatsa, and Arikara Indians.

In these treaties, the Indians acknowledged the supremacy of the United States, which in turn promised them its protection. The Indians agreed not to trade with anyone but authorized American citizens. They also agreed to the use of United States law to handle injury of American citizens by Indians and vice versa. The treaties acknowledged that the tribes lived in the United States, vowed perpetual friendship between the US and the tribes, and, recognizing the right of the United States to regulate trade, the tribes promised to deal only with licensed traders. The tribes also agreed to forswear retaliation for injuries, and to return or indemnify the owner of stolen horses or other goods. To the Indian this says the land is not theirs, it's America's land and America could control how and who they conduct their business with, as well as control retaliation and make them return stolen property. It was another "control" made by the United States over the Indians. It was signed 30 July 1825.[26]

At almost the same time, another treaty called "The Treaty of Prairie du Chien, 1825" was signed in August of that year because the Inter-tribal warfare was disrupting the fur trade and the influx of miners and squatters into Indian territories was increasing the tensions so much between the settlers and Indians, something had to be done. To ease these problems, the U.S. Government invited thousands of Indians representing all the tribes in the Upper

Mississippi to gather at Prairie du Chien during August of 1825. Territorial governors William Clark of Missouri and Lewis Cass of Michigan facilitated discussions that produced a general treaty of peace among all the tribes and established boundaries between white settlers and Native Americans. It was signed on 19 August 1825 by officials from the U.S. Government and representatives from the individual tribes that were there. Separate treaties with each individual tribe was to take place at a later date.[27] All this was to place more control over the Indians!

One of the biggest "controls" the U.S. Government placed on Indians was the Indian Removal Act of 1830, which resulted in the removal and forced march of thousands of Cherokee Indians from their homes. Under orders from President Andrew Jackson, an estimated 16,000 Cherokee Indians were forced from their homes and made to walk almost 1,000 miles to what is now Oklahoma to resettle. More than 4,000 died from hunger, exposure, and disease. Under the act, the government gave the Cherokee until May 1838 to leave their homes voluntarily. Initially, the Cherokee held their ground, hoping a new president would overrule President Jackson, but that didn't happen. The actual removal occurred between May 1838 and March 1839. The Cherokee were put in stockades in the summer of 1838 and began their trek in August 1838, 1,000 Indians at a time. The journey is remembered today as the "Trail of Tears"[28][29]

Additionally, increased traffic of emigrants along many emigrant trails, beginning in the early 1820's, heightened competition with Native Americans (Indians) for scarce resources of water and game in arid areas. With resource depletion along the trails, the Cheyenne became increasingly divided. This division reinforced the formation of the Northern Cheyenne and Southern Cheyenne. They had to have adequate territory for their different ways of sustenance.

There were not only the Mormon and California emigrant trails in the east, but in the mid-west there was the Chisholm Trail, named for Jesse Chisholm, who had built several trading posts in Western Oklahoma before the American Civil War. He and Lenape Black Beaver collected stray Texas cattle and drove them to railheads over the trail, shipping the cattle back east to feed the rapidly and every increasing population and because of the higher prices in the east than in the West. Part of that trail went from San Antonio, Texas to Abilene, Kansas, which was in Cheyenne territory. In 1866, 35,000 head of cattle were shipped out of the Abilene stockyard.

There was also the Santa Fe Trail. It connected Franklin, Missouri with Santa Fe, New Mexico. It was pioneered in 1821 by William Becknell and served as a vital commercial and military highway until the introduction of the railroad to Santa Fe. The route crossed Comancheria, the territory of the Comanches, who demanded compensation for granting passage to the trail. The Santa Fe Trail was the trail used by the military in 1846—1848 to get supplies, personnel, and equipment to Mexico during the Mexican-American War. Americans routinely assaulted the Comanches because it was unacceptable to them that they had to pay a fee to travel the trail. Soon the Comanches left the area. Although the Comanches weren't in the Treaty of 1825, the same reasoning should have applied to them, but it didn't.

The Mexican-American War was from 25 April 1846 to 2 February 1848. This war came about because of a land dispute between the Republic of Texas and Mexico. Texas seceded from Mexico in 1836 and then the new Republic of Texas and Mexico both claimed Santa Fe as part of the territory north and east of the Rio Grande. The Santa Fe Trail was used heavily by Mexicans and Americans alike for commercial reasons. Soon there were minor hostile actions between the two and that led to the War of 1846.

Horace Greeley was an American author and wrote editorials for the New York Tribune. Although some say Horace didn't make the quote, "Go West, young man, go West," he has been given credit for it. The Oxford Dictionary of Quotations gives the full quotation as, "Go West, young man, and grow up with the country," and from "Hints toward Reforms" (1850) by Horace Greeley. However, the phrase does not actually occur in that book. Nevertheless, many people took that advice and traveled west to seek their fortunes.

Horace Greeley was apparently well liked and respected by the people in my home town of Tribune. There is a town two miles west of Tribune called Horace, both towns are in Greeley County and he wrote for the New York Tribune. He took a trip to Kansas in 1872 and wrote a piece about his adventures traveling to the mid-west. He named it "Overland Journey" and sent it back to the paper to be published.[30] Whether or not he visited or came close to seeing western Kansas, or the county he was later named after, is unknown. He did travel through Atchison, Leavenworth, and Lawrence.

Horace Greeley also signed the Preemption Act of 1841 which allowed "squatters" who were living on federal government owned land to purchase up to 160 acres at a very low price (not less than $1.25 per acre) before the land was to be offered for sale to the general public. To qualify, one must be the head of the household; a single man over 21, or a widow; a citizen of the United States (or an immigrant intending to become naturalized; and a resident of the claimed land for a minimum of 14 months. To claim the land, a person had to be actively residing on the land, or working to improve the land (for a minimum of five years). If the claimant let the land remain idle for six months, the government could take the property. The Preemption Act of 1841 was utilized by many settlers in the Kansas and Nebraska Territory.

This led to the Homestead Act of 1862, which was signed into law by President Lincoln on 20 May 1862. Horace Greeley also signed this Act. The Free Soil Party of 1848—52, and the new Republican Party after 1854, demanded that the new lands opening up in the west be made available to independent farmers, rather than wealthy planters who would develop it with the use of slaves, forcing the yeomen farmers onto marginal lands.

The requirements to homestead in the Homestead Act of 1862 were similar to the requirements of the Preemption Act of 1841. This time, though, one couldn't file for a homestead exemption if he/she had ever taken up arms against the U.S. government (including freed slaves). The filing fee was eighteen dollars ($18.00). Immigrants, farmers without their own land, single women, and former slaves could all qualify. Daniel Freeman was the first person to file a claim under this new law. Of course there was a good deal of fraud going on. The government developed no systematic method to evaluate claims under the homestead acts. Land offices relied on affidavits from witnesses that the claimant had lived on the land for the required period of time and made the required improvements.

In practice, some of these witnesses were bribed or otherwise colluded with the claimant. Although no fraud, it was common practice for the eligible children of a large family to claim nearby land as soon as possible. After a few generations, a family could build up a sizable estate.[31][32] Where in this act does it allow for an Indian to file a claim? It doesn't. Most Indians at the time were not farmers and had to roam the plains to find the meat for their table. Even if they could file, they couldn't improve the land, as required. This act allowed for more whites to encroach on Indian territory...legally.

In 1840, conflicts between the Cheyenne, Comanches, Kiowa, and Plains Apache ended for a while because the tribes made an alliance with each other. The alliance allowed the Cheyenne to enter the Llano Estacado, a region in the Texas and Oklahoma panhandles and northeastern New Mexico, to hunt bison and trade. Their expansion in the south and alliance with the Kiowa led to their first raid into Mexico in 1853. The raid ended in disaster with heavy resistance from Mexican Lancers (cavalry men on horseback with a long lance as their weapon), resulting in all but three of the war party being killed.

To the north, the Cheyenne made a strong alliance with the Lakota Sioux, which allowed them to expand their territory into part of their former lands around the Black Hills. The Cheyenne managed to escape the small pox epidemics which swept across the plains from white settlements in 1837-1839 by heading into the Rocky Mountains, but they were greatly affected by the Cholera epidemic in 1849. Contact with white men was mostly light, with most contact involving mountain men, traders, explorers, treaty makers, and painters.

There were many small military forts in Colorado in the 1800's.[33] One of the places the Southern Cheyenne and Arapaho Plains Indians traded their wares (mostly buffalo robes) at was a place called Bent's Old Fort, sometimes called Bent's Fort and Fort William. It was built in 1833 in Otero County in southeastern Colorado by William and Charles Bent. (Noteworthy is the fact that a famous Cheyenne squaw, Owl Woman, who was the daughter of White Thunder, was the wife of William Bent). For much of its 16-year history, it was the only major permanent settlement on the Santa Fe Trail between Missouri and the Mexican settlements. It was an adobe fort. It was 180 feet long and 135 feet wide with walls that were 15 feet high and four feet thick. It was the strongest post at that time west of Ft. Leavenworth. It was a square structure with an open courtyard in the middle. William Bent burned it down in 1852 and relocated his trading business to his log trading post at Big Timbers, (what is now Lamar, Colorado). Its name was changed to Fort Wise in 1860 and taken over by the US Government. It was there that the Treaty of Fort Wise was signed on 18 February 1861 by the United States and a few Cheyenne and Arapaho chiefs. The Treaty established a small reservation for the Cheyenne in southeastern Colorado in exchange for the territory agreed to in the Fort Laramie Treat of 1851. Many Cheyenne did not sign the treaty, and they continued to live and hunt on their traditional grounds in the Smoky Hill and Republican basins, where there were plentiful buffalo.

In 1846, Thomas Fitzpatrick was appointed US Indian agent for the upper Arkansas and Platte River areas. His efforts to negotiate with the Northern Cheyenne, the Arapaho, and other tribes led to a great council meeting at Fort Laramie in 1851. Treaties were negotiated by a commission consisting of Fitzpatrick and David Dawson Mitchell, US Superintendent of Indian Affairs, with the Indians of the northern plains.

To reduce inter-tribal warfare on the Plains, the government officials "assigned" territories to each tribe and had them pledge mutual peace. In addition, the government secured permission to build and maintain roads for travelers and traders through Indian country on the Plains, such as the Emigrant Trail and the Santa Fe Trail, and to maintain forces to guard them. The tribes were compensated with annuities of cash and supplies for such encroachment on their territories.

The Laramie Treaty of 1851 affirmed the Cheyenne and Arapaho territory on the Great Plains between the North Platte River and the Arkansas. This territory included what is now Colorado, east of the Front Range of the Rockies and north of the Arkansas River, Wyoming, and Nebraska, south of the North Platte River, and extreme western Kansas. It is unknown how much money and supplies were given to the Indians. It probably wasn't very much and you'll notice the tribes were "assigned" territories. The territories weren't theirs and the government told them this is where you will live.

About this time, we had the two major gold rushes. The first one was in California. It began on 24 January 1848 when gold was found by James W. Marshall at Sutter's Mill in Coloma, California. All told it brought about 300,000 people to California. Approximately, half arrived by sea and half came from the east overland on the California Trail and Gila River trail. The gold seekers were called "forty-niners". This gold rush resulted in attacks on Native Americans (Indians) who were forcibly removed from their lands.

An estimated 100,000 California Indians died between 1848 and 1868, and some 4,500 of them were murdered. The huge number of forty-niners and other newcomers to the area were driving the Indians out of their traditional hunting, fishing, and food-gathering areas. To protect their homes and livelihood, some of them responded by attacking the miners. This provoked counter-attacks on Indian villages. The Indians were out-gunned and were often slaughtered. Those who escaped massacres were many times unable to survive without access to their food-gathering areas, and they starved to death.

The Indians in the California area also succumbed in large numbers to introduced diseases such as smallpox, influenza, and measles. Some estimates indicated case fatality rates of 80 to 90% during smallpox epidemics.

The Act for the Government and Protection of Indians, passed on 22 April 1850 by the California Legislature, allowed settlers to continue the practice of capturing and using Native people (Indians) as bonded workers. It also provided the basis for the enslavement and trafficking in Indian labor, particularly that of young women and children, which was carried on as a legal business enterprise. Indian villages were regularly raided to supply the demand, and young women and children were carried off to be sold, the men and remaining people often being killed in genocidal attacks.

The factors of disease, however do not minimize the tone of racial violence directed towards California Indians. Peter Burnett,

California's first governor, declared that California was a battleground between the races and that there were only two options towards California Indians, extinction or removal. California, apart from legalizing slavery for Native Americans also directly paid out $25,000 in bounties for Indian scalps with varying prices for adult male, adult female, and child sizes. California with a consortium of other new Western states stood in opposition of ratifying the eighteen treaties signed between tribal leaders and federal agents in 1851. It would be naive to say that the Indians in the mid-west did not know of the plight of the Indians on the eastern side of the country.

The mid-western Indians also had their gold rush problems. The Pikes Peak Gold Rush in Colorado began in July 1858 and lasted until the creation of the Colorado Territory on 28 Feb 1861. An estimated 100,000 gold seekers, known as the "Fifty Niners" came to the area seeking gold. Their motto was "Pikes Peak or Bust". This gold rush caused the same problems with the mid-western Indians that the California gold rush caused the east coast Indians. There was another great influx of people, all trying to live off the land. Violence was everywhere and the land suffered. Mining also caused the streams and rivers to go bad and the land itself was torn apart, making it inhospitable for agriculture and animals.

It was a time of intense turmoil in Kansas. The American Civil War was fought between 1861 and 1865. Prior to this there were groups of Pro-Slavery and groups of Anti-Slavery (abolitionist) throughout the country. States were declaring themselves Pro-Slavery or Free-State. Tensions were high due to the political leanings in each state. Kansas was no exception. There were both groups in Kansas during the middle 1850's. Kansas was trying to be a Free-State but there were pro-slavery settlers arguing their case living there as well. In 1854, the Kansas-Nebraska Act was passed. This put the "Free-Staters" in violent struggles against the "Border Ruffians". Border Ruffians would come across the Missouri State line and harass the local Free-Stater settlers. On 21 May 1856, a Sheriff Jones and a posse of 750 proslavery men raided Lawrence, Kansas, which was a Free-Stater town.

A John Brown, who had recently moved to Kansas with some of his sons was an abolitionist. He had met Frederick Douglas in 1849. Frederick Douglas was an African-American social reformer, abolitionist and statesman that had escaped slavery in Maryland and had become a national leader of the abolitionist movement. He was noted for his gifted oratory and anti-slavery writings. He was also the first African-American invited into the White House. Meeting Douglas sealed John Brown's belief in being an abolitionist.

When John Brown heard of the Lawrence raid, he and his sons and a few other men tried to retaliate. On 21 May 1856, they ended up killing five pro-settlers that were living on the Pottawatomie Creek. They pulled them out of their homes in the dead of night, took them a few hundred yards from their house, and murdered them violently with sabers. One was, reportedly, shot in the head by John Brown himself. They left them lay where they killed them. These killings became rapidly known about.

It put fear in many settlers and increased the tensions in Kansas considerably. When Henry Pate heard about the killings, he organized a small pro-slavery militia force and set out after John Brown. Pate found and captured two of Brown's sons and then

ROBERT PETERSON

found Brown and his small force near Baldwin City, Kansas. A skirmish took place for several hours, resulting in a few more deaths and wounded, and resulted in Pate's surrender. This skirmish, or battle as it became known as, was then called the Battle of Black Jack.[34] It is significant in that it was covered in most of the countries newspapers as being a battle between pro-slavery against anti-slavery forces. The newspaper articles also introduced John Brown, who was saying that there should be an armed conflict to end slavery. This battle site is also significant as some historians are calling it the first battle of the Civil War. In 2012, the battle site was designated a National Historic Landmark.

On 30 August 1856, just a few months later, John Brown and about 40 of his men tried to defend the town of Osawatomie, Kansas from some 250-400 Border Ruffians. There were just too many ruffians for John Brown's men to adequately defend the town. There were numerous casualties and Brown's forces had to withdraw. John Brown would not stop here. On 16 October, 1859, he attacked the Federal Armory at Harper's Ferry in Virginia. He thought he could seize the 100,000 weapons stored there by the Union Army and continue his fight by using the weapons seized in a guerrilla type war in the Blue Ridge Mountains. Most of John Brown's forces were killed. John Brown was captured in the Armory fire engine house (now known as "John Brown's Fort" by some U. S. Marines commanded by Col. Robert E. Lee and Lieutenant J.E.B. Stuart, both who later became famous Confederate Generals.

John Brown was brought to trial and found guilty of treason because he conspired with slaves to rebel and murder. He was hanged on 2 December 1859.[35] Again, his fight, trial, and subse-

34

quent hanging made the news. It brought the nation's attention to the struggle between those opposed and those for slavery. This battle triggered the Civil War, even though the war had not officially started yet. It should be noted that Kansas, shortly thereafter, became a Free state in 1861.

In 1863, more violence and killings came to Kansas. There was the the burning of Lawrenceville, Kansas by William Quantrill's Raiders. His group was pro-slavery and they attacked and burned the City of Lawrenceville Kansas, which was anti-slavery. The mayor of the city had previously had all the weapons in the city confiscated and stored. No one was armed. When Quantrill raided the city he and his men shot and killed over 200 unarmed men. They ransacked the city and burned most of it down. Kansas became to be known as "Bleeding Kansas" due to all the killings and violence. This was in addition to all the Indian problems the settlers in Kansas were already experiencing.

In 1863, even with the Civil War going on, American entrepreneurs saw the American Southwest as a way to make money. This led to the construction east to west of the Atchison, Topeka, and Santa Fe Railway, which, again, was through Indian territory.

The travel westward by people heightened the need for a railroad to go to the West Coast. In 1863, the groundbreaking ceremony for the western leg of the First Transcontinental Railroad was held in Sacramento. The lines completion, some six years later, financed in part with Gold Rush money, united California with the central and eastern United States. No surprise here that that it ran through Indian territory.

There were many animals on the Kansas plains that seemed to love the heat and shear vastness of the open plains, especially the antelope, deer, coyote, and buffalo. Although there were at one time vast herds of buffalo, they were becoming somewhat scare due to the white man over-hunting them. It has been estimated that there were 50 — 60 million buffalo roaming the plains at one time. To make matters worse the white man even hired men to kill the Indian's "sacred buffalo." They did it for various reasons.

Buffalo meat was used extensively to feed the soldiers at the Army Posts that were now springing up in the West. Buffalo meat was also used to feed the construction workers that were working on the "iron horse" rail lines. Killing the buffalo also kept them away, for safety reasons, from the railroad lines that were now crossing the prairies. The trains couldn't travel through the uncontrolled herds of buffalo if they were on the train tracks. Another reason was to sell their hides to be used in coats and other items such as lap robes when riding in sleighs and carriages. Some tanneries, such as the one in Fort Leavenworth, made belts for industrial machines and ground the bones into fertilizer. Some hunters killed buffalo for the money. They could get as much as $3.00 per hide and 25 cents for their tongues, which were considered a delicacy in fine restaurants. This was good money for them and attracted many hunters.

It was estimated that there were as many as 5,000 buffalo hunters in the 1800's. Armed with long rifles, a hunter could shoot and kill around 250 buffalo a day. And the worse reason of all was for the sport of it. It got so bad that some of the hunters simply shot the buffalo for fun from a train as it rolled along the track, leaving the buffalo behind to rot. And some of the buffalo hunters such as Bill Tilghman and William "Buffalo Bill" Cody became famous doing it. They were, however, at the same time destroying the herds the Indians needed to survive.[36]

One such hunter was a Charles Rath. The following is an article entitled "Charles Rath, Buffalo Hunter" from Early Ford County, by Ida Ellen Rath, Dodge City, KS. It is quoted below: [37]

> "On the wide, windswept plains of the Western Kansas and the Panhandle of Texas, hunters followed and shot the shaggy, humpbacked transient herds of bison. Their slaughter brought about a great industrial drama that culminated in the practical extinction of the buffalo, the end of Indian warfare, and the rush of settlers to populate the plains.
>
> Shoot them they did, courageous, adventuresome, expert marksmen to the tune of nearly two million a year and thereby lined their pockets with "buffalo gold." Few of these old buffalo hunters survive today, but the fruits of their industry are still living monuments.
>
> But many are the men who shot the buffalo still living on in the annals of history; in the innermost recesses of your heart and mine. A goodly number of those early day hunters, the first family men of Dodge City, invested their buffalo gold into businesses of their own or enabled others to do so; the fruits of their industry monuments to early day men and their truly pioneering wives.
>
> Reams have been written about early day buffalo hunters who later became famous for various reasons, namely: Wyatt Earp, Bill Tilghman, "Bat" Masterson, "Buffalo Bill" Cody. But many other hunters were as expert on the draw and as widely known throughout the buffalo range. Mention buffalo

hunters, of whom there were thousands, and memories of some of the great buffalo hunters spring into the limelight again: Charley Rath and his helper, Andy Johnson; "Brick" Bond; Bill Gillespie; George Bellfield; George Reighard; "Texas Jack" Mathias; and one other, "Prairie Dog Dave" Morrow of the white buffalo fame.

In the sixties and almost through the seventies, great migrating herds of hump-backed, shaggy buffalo darkened the plains as far as the eye could reach. They fed on the succulent buffalo and grama grass whether it was green in summer or dry in winter. They drank from creeks, rivers, and "buffalo wallows," depressions made in the hard-packed alkaline soil by buffalo licking the salt from the ground. Little groups of grazing buffalo, their tangled dewlaps almost dragging the ground, combined to make one vast herd which was always on the move during that instinctive migration which drove them north in summer, south in the winter.

In 1872, before the arrival of the Santa Fe railroad at Buffalo City, later re-named Dodge City, the buffalo had been killed mostly to provide food and hides for present needs by white man and Indian alike, Hays City did have a hide market previous to this time, however, and many hides were shipped from that point. But, with the coming of the railroad, many a man laid down the tools of this trade to shoot the buffalo; many would-be hunters were so young they had no trade; many were seasoned trappers and Indian traders even though their youth belied the fact.

Charles Rath was from Sweetwine, Ohio, but "Plainsman Charley" as early as 1853, foresaw great possibilities in the opened market in the east, not only for buffalo hides and other furs, but for choice buffalo tongue, fat-streaked hump, and delicious steak. As a boy of twelve, while waiting with his parents for clearance at the custom house, Charley Rath had been teased by other children because he wore his brother's outgrown suit, fully four sizes too large, its lines sagging shabbily on the lean youth. If those children could have looked into the future, at one of the first family men in Dodge City, this boy turned man, they would have seen a large man with a head of black hair topped with a fine beaver hat, clothed in a rich brown tailor-made suit and shirt. His button shoes were shining black and his gloves were white. In later years, a niece of Mr. Rath wrote her cousin Robert, "I remember well the occasional visits of your father to our home when we were children to whom he seemed a fairy prince driving a prancing livery team and carrying a big bag of goodies for the children."

When Charles Rath accompanied his high Conestoga freight wagons, it was a common sight during rest periods, to see the great man ensconced safely under a wagon-tongue, its end held high by the propped neck yoke. In the shade of the wagon, the grown man improved his education from the supply of text books which he always considered a necessary part of camp equipment."

As the slaughter of the buffalo continued, the Indians became increasingly angry and resentful as they watched their main source of sustenance dwindle at the hands of the white man. This led to more and more Indian attacks which resulted in the Army's retaliation, which led to the Indian wars. The Army aggressively pursued a policy to eradicate the buffalo intentionally which would extinguish the Indians sustenance and help the US Government separate the Indians from the rest of "civilization" and place them in reservations.

Even General Philip Sheridan defended the buffalo hunters and opposed a Texas Legislature bill to protect the buffalo. Gen. Sheridan said, "These men have done more in the last two years, and will do more in the next year, to settle the vexed Indian question, than the entire regular army has done in the last forty years. They are destroying the Indians' commissary. And it is a well-known fact that an army losing its base of supplies is placed at a great disadvantage. Send them powder and lead, if you will; but for a lasting peace, let them kill, skin, and sell until the buffaloes are exterminated. Then your prairies can be covered with speckled cattle."

There was a great demand for meat, especially beef. The great Civil War between the North and the South was over in 1865 and back east the population increase alone was causing a big demand for beef. Cattle were now driven on round-ups to the nearest train depot to be shipped back east to meet the demand. Small cities and towns were beginning to crop up in western Kansas and there was a large influx of settlers/farmers to the area as well. The settlers and farmers would kill antelope and deer for meat, as well as their own cattle. The wild animals were still there but it was getting harder and harder to find them and even harder, if not impossible, to survive solely on the meat they provided.

Apparently a lot of buffalo were killed in Greeley County as well. An article in a 2013 issue of the Greeley County Republican quotes a Clyde Blackburn from Leoti, Kansas who was giving a speech to the Greeley County Rotary Club. The article states, "He mentioned Masterson, Gov. St. John, and Clarkson hunting buffalo along the Beaver in Greeley County. Clarkson killed 7,000 at one site."[38]

It's not hard to see why the Native Indians were so upset with the white man!

Part 2: First Battle (Solomon River)

In Europe, fighting men on horseback were called "Dragoons". At one time America also used that name for its mounted riflemen. In 1833, the "First Regiment of Dragoons" was formed and soon after that the "Second Regiment of Dragoons" was formed. It stayed that way until 1855 and the two Regiments were re-named the 1st Cavalry Regiment and the 2nd Cavalry Regiment at Jefferson Barracks, MO. They were the first Army units to be designated as "Cavalry". Then, in 1860, they were re-named the 4th and 5th Cavalry Regiments and the army formed two more cavalry units and designated them as the 1st and 2nd Cavalry Regiments.

Each regiment was commanded by a full colonel with a lieutenant colonel as 2nd in command with 2 majors as staff officers. Each regiment had ten (10) companies commanded by a captain. Also in each company there was one first lieutenant, one second lieutenant, four sergeants, four corporals, and eighty-four privates. Attached to each company was one farrier (blacksmith) and two buglers. That makes each company have 98 cavalrymen. There were 10 companies so that comes to 980 cavalrymen plus the lieutenant colonel and his 2 majors for a total of 983 cavalry-men in each regiment.

This number of cavalrymen doesn't address the staff that had to support each regiment. There were cooks, medics, etc. that went with each regiment. When on the move, it was an awesome sight. There were many covered wagons carrying supplies, chuck wagons for the cooks, and a remuda of spare horses and several hundred cattle.

The regiment had four field grade officers (majors or above) and one half of the company grade officers (captains and lieutenants) were to come from existing army units. The other half of the company grade officers and most of the enlisted men came from civilian life. Each company sent out one lieutenant and one sergeant to city after city to recruit men to fill the ranks. Posters, displayed in each city promised good clothing, rations, and medical attention. The pay rate was $12.00 a month for privates, $14.00 for corporals, $17.00 for Duty Sergeants, and $22.00 for First Sergeants. Once recruited, after a physical exam, the new recruits were then trained in horsemanship and as cavalrymen at Fort Leavenworth and Jefferson Barracks.

Each company had horses of a distinctive color. This served two purposes. In addition to the dramatic effect on parade, the distinctive color made it easy for members of the regiment to locate their company in the heat of battle. The assigned colors were Company A had sorrels; B, grays; C, sorrels; D, bays; E, roans; F, sorrels; G, blacks; H, bays; I sorrels; and, K, bays. The buglers had white horses. The officers each had two horses. They could select the color of their choice. Officers were required to provide their own uniforms, equipment, and horses.

In 1855, one of the initial missions of the 1st Cavalry Regiment was to maintain the peace in the Kansas Territory between the pro-slavery group who fought to make the territory a slave state, and the free-state faction, who bitterly opposed them. This conflict helped give rise to and support the "Bleeding Kansas" mentality. However, in April 1856, an incident at the Platte River Bridge (near present-day Casper, Wyoming), which resulted in the wounding of a Cheyenne warrior brought about another mission for the 1st Cavalry. The wounded Cheyenne warrior returned to the tribe and apparently stirred up a ruckus because the Cheyenne, who had been peaceful, were now angry.

During the summer of 1856, Indians (possibly Cheyenne) attacked travelers along the Emigrant Trail near Fort Kearny, Nebraska. Then Cheyenne war parties attacked four wagon trains, killing twelve people and kidnapping two. In retaliation, the US Cavalry attacked a Cheyenne camp on Grand Island in Nebraska. They killed ten Cheyenne warriors and wounded eight or more. After this action, the Commander of the Department of the West recommended the Cheyenne be punished for their attacks on emigrant trains. However, he recommended that any action be put off until the spring of 1857.

In May 1857, preparation began for the campaign against the Cheyenne. The Secretary of War ordered the 1st Cavalry Regiment under the command of Colonel Edwin V. Sumner to carry out a punitive expedition against them. Col. Sumner divided the regiment into two columns in order to circle the Cheyenne hunting grounds in central Kansas Territory. One column, under Major John Sedgwick, departed on May 18 with four companies, five Delaware scouts, and forty wagons, heading west along the Arkansas River past Bent's Fort, north to the South Fork of the Platte River. There they were to meet Sumner's column, which had left Fort Leavenworth on May 20, with four cavalry companies, 300 cattle, and 51 wagons. Sumner's column went north and then west up to Fort Kearny, where three companies of the 6th Infantry Regiment and two companies of the 1st Cavalry Regiment (formerly the 2nd Dragoons), five Pawnee scouts, and ten more wagons were added. After considerable difficulty in crossing the South Platte River, Sumner's column and Sedgwick's columns met at the South Platte as planned on July 4th. The whole regiment then traveled east through central Kansas to their rendezvous with the Cheyenne on the Solomon River with a combined force of about 400 troops/cavalrymen.

Meanwhile, the Cheyenne, about three hundred strong, were midway between the two columns, probably around the Republican River, where they had spent the previous winter. The Cheyenne consisted of both Northern Cheyenne and Southern Cheyenne. They knew the U.S. Cavalry was searching for them, so they remained banded together longer than they normally did. Under the influence of the medicine man, White Bull (also called Ice) and Grey Beard (also called Dark), the Cheyenne went into battle believing that strong spiritual medicine would prevent the soldier's guns from firing. They were told that if they dipped their hands in a nearby lake, they had only to raise their hands to repel army bullets.

On July 29, 1857, the U.S. 1st Cavalry Regiment caught up with the Cheyenne on the bank of the Solomon River. The two groups paused within about a mile of each other. The Cheyenne raised their hands as the cavalry moved toward them. Then Col. Sumner gave the command "Gallop march". The Cheyenne also galloped toward the cavalrymen. Then Col. Sumner gave the commands of "Sling carbines! Draw Sabers! Charge!". It was the first time sabers had been used in the West. The astonished Cheyenne, thinking they were protected from bullets but not sabers, were terrified. They turned and fled on horseback.

The Cavalrymen chased after them for about seven miles but the Cheyenne horses were fresh and faster and easily outran the charging Cavalrymen. During the brief battle before the Cheyenne fled, only two Cavalrymen were killed and nine were wounded. One of the wounded was Lt. J.E.B. Stuart, who was later to become the Confederates most famous cavalry general during the Civil War. Lt. Stuart was shot in the breast while attacking a Cheyenne warrior with his saber. Nine Cheyenne warriors were killed and a few were wounded.[39][40]

This was the first battle the Cheyenne fought against the US Army. After the battle, the cavalry continued searching for them. They found a large hastily abandoned Cheyenne camp two days later. They destroyed the lodges and the Indian's winter supply of buffalo meat. Col. Sumner continued to Bent's Fort. To punish the Cheyenne even more he gave their annuities from a previous treaty to the Arapaho. He wanted to punish the Cheyenne more but the Army ordered him to Utah because of trouble there with the Mormons. This became known as the Utah War. The Cheyenne returned to their territory north of the Platte.

Part 3: 2nd Battle (Battle Of Sand Creek)

The Cheyenne were victims of their large size, for factions within their nation were poorly understood by the American settlers encroaching on their territories. For years, relations between Cheyenne Indians and white Americans followed an ugly pattern of some settler killing a Cheyenne woman from one clan, that clan killing some settlers in revenge, and then angry soldiers killing some bewildered Cheyennes from a different band/clan—prompting their own kin to take revenge and starting the cycle anew. This cycle reached its worst point in the Sand Creek massacre of 1864.

In the 1850's, tensions were high between the Indians and the US Government and the ever-expanding settlers on the mid-western plains. After the battle with the Cheyenne in 1857 and the problems the Pikes Peak Gold Rush were causing, the Cheyenne and Arapahos both started attacking wagon trains, mining camps, and stagecoach lines. As this violence continued to escalate, the Territorial Governor of Colorado, John Evans, became more and more angry with the Indians. In 1864, he sent for Colonel John Chivington, who was the Commander of the Colorado Volunteers, a rag tag citizens militia. He told Chivington to quiet the Indians. Colonel Chivington was once a member of the clergy. However, he had no compassion for Indians, which was well documented.

In 1864, the Civil War was raging in the eastern and southeastern part of the United States. This didn't deter Colonel Chivington. He started a campaign of violence against the Cheyenne and their allies. His troops attacked any and all Indians and razed their villages. The Cheyenne then joined with the Arapho, Sioux, Commanche, and Kiowa and went on a defense warpath in Colorado and Kansas. Colonel Chivington and his troops killed any Indian on sight. His unit's actions were so bad that it precipitated the Colorado War, which was a war of whites vs Indians. Much of it centered on Indian raids on the trail along the South Platte which Denver depended on for supplies. It was so bad that the Army closed the trail/road from August 15 until September 24, 1864. The war continued to escalate. Governor Evans and Colonel Chivington reinforced their militia, raising the Third Colorado Cavalry, which was made up of short-term volunteers who referred to themselves as the "Hundred Dazers."

That summer there were small raids and clashes all over the Colorado/Kansas territories by both Colonel Chivington and the Indians. Finally, the Cheyenne and Arapaho were ready for peace. They sent an Indian representative to meet with Major Edward Wynkoop [41] at Fort Lyon on the Arkansas.

The Southern Cheyenne's leader, Chief Black Kettle, turned four white captives over to Wynkoop and promised to live peacefully on a reservation. Major Wynkoop then took Chief Black Kettle to meet with Colonel Chivington and Govenor Evans on 28 September at Camp Weld, just outside of Denver. Colonel Chivington invited them to establish a camp near Fort Lyon. There were nearly 230 Indian lodges of Cheyenne and Arapaho Indians there to accept or refuse the terms given them. Some of them believed that camping near army posts they would be declaring peace and accepting sanctuary and peace could be had. However, no treaty was signed because some of the Cheyenne and Arapaho still distrusted the white man.

Those Cheyenne that didn't want to sign a treaty and that still distrusted the white man left and went north to join up with the Sioux. The remainder of the Cheyenne and Arapaho set up camp in early November at a place known as Sand Creek. It was set up there because of their need to hunt game and that was a good spot and it was under the protection of Fort Lyon. Chief Black Kettle's group of Indians set up more than 100 of their lodges along the creek. There were around 550 total Indians that set up camp there at that time.

However, upon hearing about Colonel Chivington's peace talk with the Indians and what had transpired, General Samuel Curtis, Colonel Chivington's superior officer, sent him a telegram saying, "I want no peace till the Indians suffer more…No peace must be made without my directions." This arrived and was given to Colonel Chivington on the day of the peace talks. This pleased Chivington because he hated the Indians and he had just formed up the Third Colorado Cavalry of volunteers for 100 days and had promised them an Indian war. So, Colonel Chivington lied to the Indians, promising them peace while all along he was planning on attacking and eliminating them.

Then on 29 November 1864, Colonel Chivington and his forces attacked Chief Black Kettle's Cheyennes at Sand Creek. Colonel Chivington led his 700 troops to Sand Creek and positioned them, as well as their four howitzers, for the attack. Many of the troopers were drinking heavily. They were now getting their promised "Indian war". Chief Black Kettle saw them setting up and raised an American flag and a white flag over his teepee in a sign of friendship. It did not stop Chivington's volunteers. They began to pound the village with cannon and rifle fire. The Indians scattered in panic. The frenzied and drunken Third Colorado Cavalry rode in and attacked. A few warriors managed to fight back, allowing some of the others to escape across the stream.

The cavalry continued to assault the village for most of the day. Numerous atrocities were committed. One lieutenant was said to have killed and scalped three women and five children who had surrendered and were screaming for mercy. After chasing the fleeing Indians for a while, they stopped and returned to the camp and continued killing all the wounded they could find and taking scalps off everyone, to include the women and children. When the attack was over, 70-163 Indians were killed and many were mutilated. Most of them were old men, women, children, and babies. The cavalry only lost nine or ten men, with about three dozen wounded. They then plundered the teepees and divided up the Indian's horses.

One man, Silas Soule, a Massachusetts abolitionist, refused to follow Colonel Chivington's orders. He did not allow his cavalry company to fire into the Indian camp.

Black Kettle and his wife followed the others up the stream bed. He escaped. She was shot nine times and left for dead, but somehow she survived. The survivors, over half of whom were wounded, sought refuge in the camp of the Cheyenne Dog Warriors, who had remained opposed to the peace negotiation.

The Third Colorado Cavalry returned to Denver after the Sand Creek massacre. Colonel Chivington went on stage in Denver and displayed 100 scalps, including the pubic hairs of women to the delight of the crowd. They were treated as heroes by everyone in the Colorado Territory until, that is, eyewitnesses reported what actually happened at Sand Creek. An investigation was ordered by the US Congress. At the investigation, Colonel Chivington was asked why he killed children. He replied, "Nits make lice."

Silas Soule testified against Colonel Chivington at the investigation. After he testified, however, he was murdered by Charles W. Squires, a murder believed to have been ordered by Colonel Chivington. Because of the investigation, Colonel Chivington was forced to resign but no one was ever punished or prosecuted for the massacre or the murder of Silas Soule. [42] [43] [44]

The Sand Creek battle site was authorized as a National Historic site on August 2, 2005. One can take tours of the site today. [45] [46]

Part 4: Battle Of Washita River & Battle Of Little Big Horn

Shortly after the Sand Creek Massacre, about 1000 Cheyenne and Arapho warriors carried out an attack in January 1865 on Camp Rankin, a stage station and fort at Julesburg, Colorado in retaliation for the Sand Creek Massacre.

Camp Rankin was originally named the Post at Julesburg Station. It was renamed Camp Rankin in 1864 and later changed to Fort Rankin in 1865. The Indians continued to make raids along the South Platte and Overland Trail, both east and west of Julesburg. Some of these raids were given names: Battle of Mud Springs, Battle of Rush Creek, and the Battle of Platte Bridge.

Also in January 1865, the Indians raided a small Overland stage station/rest stop and grocery store for travelers located at Merino, Colorado. The rest stop was owned and operated by a Holon and Matilda Godfrey. There were about 300 Indians that tried to burn them out and massacre them, but the Godfrey's, along with three other men, tenaciously fought back and survived the attack. Afterward, the Cheyenne Indians nicknamed the station Fort Wicked because of the fighting spirit of the station's agent, Holon Godfrey, who refused to give up and who the Indians now called, "Old Wicked."[47][48] This was the only station in the region not captured or destroyed during the January 1865 Indian raids. There is a historical monument located on US 6 south of the town today.

The Cheyenne raided Julesburg (Rankin) again a month later in February 1865. This time they captured a lot of loot and killed many European Americans. After that, most of the Indians moved north into Nebraska on their way to the Black Hills and the Powder River.

Chief Black Kettle, who had escaped at the Battle of Sand Creek, was in on the first raid at Camp Rankin. He did not go on any of the other raids after that. He was still trying to promote peace with the white man. He left the other Indians and camped his small band of about 80 lodges of his tribesmen near the Arkansas River. Although Black Kettle's band was camped on a defined Indian reservation, complying with the government's order, some of his warriors had been linked to raiding parties into Kansas. It appears that although Chief Black Kettle wanted peace for his band, it appears he couldn't control all his warriors. Consequently, four years after the Battle of Sand Creek, on November 27, 1868, General George Armstrong Custer and his troops attacked Black Kettle's band at the Battle of Washita River. This battle occurred in what is now Oklahoma. General Custer and his men of the 7th Cavalry killed Chief Black Kettle and more than 100 Cheyenne, however, most of those killed were women and children.

The Indians got their revenge against General Custer later. Several thousand Sioux, Arapaho, Lakota and Cheyenne warriors killed General Custer in what is known as the "Battle of the

Little Bighorn" and commonly called "Custer's last stand". The Lakota Indians refer to the battle as the "Battle of the Greasy Grass". This occurred on 25 and 26 June 1876 in Big Horn County, Montana. The Indian leaders were Sitting Bull (a Sioux), Crazy Horse, Chief Gall, Lame White Man, and Two Moon.

Once again, the cause of the war/battle was the U.S. Government. The government wanted the ownership of the Black Hills. Gold had been discovered and settlers were encroaching onto the Native American lands and the Sioux and the Cheyenne refused to cede ownership to the United States. Traditionally, the major conflicts were between the Sioux and the U.S. Government due to the large amount of Sioux involved. However, some historians now believe the Cheyenne Indians were the major target of the U.S. Government due to past problems with the Cheyenne and that it should really be called "The Great Cheyenne War". "The Great Sioux War" took place during the presidencies of Ulysses S. Grant and Rutherford B. Hayes. The Agreement of 1877 officially "annexed" Sioux land and 454 "PERMANENTLY" established Indian reservations.

It's interesting to note that General Custer had command of Companies I, F, C, E and L that day and there were no survivors in those companies. General Custer had assigned three of the other companies to Captain Frederick Benteen and three more to Major Reno. Company B was in charge of the rear guard and pack escort. There were survivors in these companies. The last Caucasian/7th Cavalry survivor of the Battle of the Little Bighorn, a Charles Windolph, died on March 11, 1950 at Lead, South Dakota. He had been in Company H. Forty-five (45) years after he retired from the Seventh Cavalry, he received his Congressional

Medal of Honor. Apparently, he had been cited for it earlier but the paperwork was mislaid in the War Department for 52 years.[49]

Also noteworthy is the fact that a horse, named Comanche, who had belonged to Captain Myles Keough, survived the attack. While he has been heralded as the lone survivor of the battle, many historians believe that as many as 100 horses survived and were either captured by the Indians or bolted during the battle. Comanche had no less than seven bullet wounds during the battle. The Indians had no use for a horse that was wounded and perhaps that's why the Indians didn't take him.

Comanche was initially taken to Fort Abraham Lincoln in the Dakota Territory, nursed back to health, and was officially retired from service in April 1878. The commanding officer of the fort ordered that "a special and comfortable stall is fitted for him, and he will not be ridden by any person whatever, under any circumstances nor will he be put to any kind of work." Comanche then toured the country for a while. The public loved him. He was a favorite of parades and patriotic gatherings. The public thought that he was General Custer's horse. This was fine with the government because they wanted the public on their side while they killed Indians.[50][51]

Comanche was later stabled at Fort Riley, Kansas. He was given the honorary title of "second in command" of the 7th Cavalry and he lived out his days as a company mascot. He died of colic on November 7, 1891 and by a quirk of circumstances he was stuffed and is now on display in a glass case at the University of Kansas' Natural History Museum, the Dyche Museum of Natural History. The case used to have a brass plaque: "Sole survivor of the Battle of Little Big Horn." It was removed in the 1970s at the request of local tribes.

After the Washita Battle, there was no peace with the white man by the Cheyenne for many years. The white man just couldn't be trusted and the things he did in battle were not honorable.

Fifty years after the Battle of the Little Bighorn, survivors gathered in Montana. The men, including 82-year-old Brig. Gen. Edward S. Godfrey, Cheyenne Indians, and other veterans assembled in June 1926 to shake hands, honor their lost, and ritually bury the tomahawk of the aging Sioux Chief White Bull.

3. WARRIORS AT THE CREEK

TON O KON (DARK WATER) AND WAC BEY (SILVER STAR) HAD ridden their horses a long way and they, and their horses, were tired. They had stopped on a small rise and were looking over the flat and slightly rolling plains in front of them. They had dismounted and were standing by their horses. They were taking in all they could see in the hopes they would see some wild life to kill and take back to their tribe of Cheyenne. They were also looking for water so they could let their horses drink and cool down.

It was the summer of 1868 and it was a typical hot western Kansas summer afternoon. The sun's heat was intense, bringing the temperature to a scorching 105 degrees. The only things moving on the plains during this time of day normally were jackrabbits, tumbleweeds, and heat waves waving in the air above the parched land. At mid-day on the plains, both man and beast tended to sit or lie down and try to endure the heat the best way they knew how. Most of the animals would hunker down in their burrows or holes in the ground until the heat of the day would pass. Some would try and find shade, although it was difficult to do because of the lack of trees and other types of vegetation that could provide adequate shade.

On the other hand, humans would simply sit where they were and stop doing what they had been doing and wait out the hottest hours of the afternoon. Once the sun's rays started to abate a little, they would continue doing what they had been doing, normally until dusk. For the few farmers that were in the area, it would just get too hot to work their animals and expect them to work all day in the heat without stopping for a while and hydrating them. Otherwise the animals, be they oxen, cows, or horses, would tire and couldn't work at peak performance. The same reasoning applied to the farmer. He had to stop and hydrate himself as well. He could easily have a heat stroke. While the animals were drinking their water and resting, farmers would often sit in the animal's shade, since there were, normally, no trees in the field, and try to cool down. He could also better control the animals by being close to them.

It was mid-day and hot. The two Cheyenne warriors stared out over the horizon and all they could see were the heat waves and a small plumb of smoke in the distance, possibly coming from one of the many homesteads that were fast spreading across the open prairies. A whirlwind suddenly started to develop off to the west of them about a mile away. The whirlwind known to the farmers as "dust devils" were a small, swirling amount of wind that looked like the beginning of a tornado. However, they didn't amount to much and would simply stir up some dust and prairie debris and after a few minutes would dissipate and cease to exist. They didn't amount to much but were a nuisance when you got into one.

The two warriors were dressed in their normal Indian garments. They were wearing moccasins, a breechcloth with leather leggings and leather vests that had numerous beads on the side of them. Nothing fancy. They were just beads that had been randomly put on by one of the tribal squaws. They were on a scouting mission for meat, preferably buffalo. They were not looking for trouble from anyone or anything. Their hair was long, stretching down almost to their waists. It was custom for them to keep their hair long. It was considered to be an extension of the soul. Therefore, taking scalps was believed to hinder entering the afterworld. It was braided in two braids, one on each side of their head and the braids were hanging in front of them on their chests. Neither had a head band or feather stuck in his hair.

Both carried a bow and a quiver of arrows looped over their head and one shoulder. Dark Water also had a Model 1866, .45 caliber, Springfield Carbine in his left hand and a small pouch on his waist that had 20 rifle shells in it. Silver Star was also carrying a Model 1866, .45 caliber, Winchester repeating rifle and had 30 rifle shells in his pouch. Neither of them were carrying pistols.

Although they still had spears, the two of them had stopped carrying them when they carried their rifles. Their early spear tips were made of bone but now their spear tips were of copper or iron. They still used spears when hunting buffalo from time to time but it was more of a tradition than anything with them. They used the heavy spears on the hunts because they caused maximum damage at a safe distance. They also took the spears with them on big game hunts in case their rifles misfired or jammed and wouldn't fire. And this happened often due to poor maintenance of their rifles and ammo. Then they reverted to using their spears and bows and arrows. The heavy spears were used on big game hunts in order to bring down the big game such as buffalos, deer, and elk. Smaller spears were used by the warriors in warfare with other Indians.[52]

There was no saddle on the horses and they were being ridden using an old leather rein. It had no bit and was only on one side of the horse's neck. The two warriors were excellent riders and they guided their horses by mostly using their legs and feet and a soft pull on the rein.

The horses were hot and sweaty after being ridden for so long in the overpowering heat, but they were still hungry and trying to graze as the two Cheyenne warriors stood there.

Both warriors were also prominently carrying their sacred bundle. "The bundle" was a small bag made of buffalo skin and it contained a hat made from a buffalo hide and four arrows. Two of the arrows were painted for hunting and two were painted for battle. This bundle was carried by all Cheyenne warriors into war and on hunts to ensure success.

With small beads of sweat dripping off his forehead, Dark Water pointed toward a wisp of smoke in the distance. He looked at Silver Star and said calmly, "White man." Silver Star simply acknowledged him with a "Hmmmmm" and a nod of his head. Both knew the white man and both had learned from their tribal elders and personal experience with the white man to distrust and dislike him. Although the Cheyenne Indians had been, and some still were, peaceful Indians, they had many reasons for their hatred of the white man ... and some Indians. Dark Water and Silver Star had to be on the alert at all times.

The two warriors are mentioned to illustrate the fact that Indians were still freely roaming the plains in sometimes large numbers during this period and to point out that the settlers had

THE GHOST OF WHITE WOMAN CREEK

to be aware of their presence and take the necessary steps to protect themselves.

Also, to illustrate the fact that there was water in White Woman Creek, at least from time to time, there is a painting of Indians stopping and letting their horses drink water from the creek in the September/October 2015 Issue of the Saturday Evening Post. The artist of the painting is Howard Terpning, who is a well-known artist of western and Indian people and activities.[53] He has the original on display in his art gallery. It is titled, "Cheyenne at the Disappearing Creek." It is a 28 x 35 painting on Giclee Canvas and prints of it are for sale.[54]

Cheyenne at the Disappearing Creek Called White Woman by Howard Terpning © Terpning Family Limited Partnership, LLLP All Rights Reserved.

According to a pamphlet titled, "And Greeley County Began", by Margaret Pile, the creek was originally called, "Poison

Creek". It is unknown why it had that name. One can assume that it was called Poison Creek because it was so polluted and contaminated at one time and in certain areas that perhaps it had killed some of the local wildlife like coyotes, badgers, buffalo, and maybe even some of the settlers livestock.[55]

White Woman Creek is a small creek that forms in the eastern part of Colorado near Cheyenne Wells and Arapahoe, Colorado. It then runs southeasterly through the southern part of Wallace County, Kansas and then through Greeley County, Kansas at which time it tends to flow more easterly and travel through Leoti, Kansas (Wichita County) and ends up draining in a relatively flat basin in Scott County, just south of Scott City, Kansas.

Because the creek was mostly a dry creek bed, it made Greeley County the only county in the state that didn't have a running stream in it in the 1880's.[56] It had, at one time, been a creek that had water in it most of the time, as evidenced by Terpning's painting. Evidence of its continual water supply is gained also from the artifacts found all along the creek bed and its nearby banks. There have been numerous bones of wild animals and even a Mastodon's skull and mandible unearthed in Greeley County, which is on display in the Greeley County, Kansas museum.[57] Numerous arrow heads and other Indian artifacts have also been found and are on display in the museum also.

Additionally, an article in the History of Early Greeley County, Vol. 1 written by Mrs. Grace Hougland Bjork, titled Ft. Wallace-Ft. Lyons Trail, (Barrel Springs Northwest) locates Barrel Springs (part of White Woman Creek) as being 10 miles west and four miles north of Tribune in Colony Township, about a mile down the creek from the Raymond Estes home.[58] In the early days, some traveler sank two barrels into the north bank of the stream just across from the hole known now to many as the Jumbo hole. Here the spring flowed into the barrels and out into the creek bed. So, the spring was given the name "Barrel Springs". According to Mrs. Bjork the Jumbo hole was used by many of the locals as a swimming hole. At one time, it was measured and found to be 14 feet deep at the south end.

Further, Mrs. Nadine Cheney, also wrote an article in the History of Early Greeley County, Vol. 1, titled Dead Horse Lake, in which she tells of the water supply in the local area. She stated that Dead Horse Lake is located in the southwest part of Greeley County, and has a considerable drainage area. Now dry, but when full it could cover approximately 250 acres.[59] She also says that research has shown that when the area was all native grass, Dead Horse Lake could possibly have held water year round. So, it can be deduced that Indians traveled frequently in this area and along this creek, and a creek just north of it called Ladder Creek, (See Fig #1 Map, which shows White Woman Creek and Ladder Creek meandering route) because of their water supply. It was also a possible source of food and water for both the homesteaders and Indians alike, which, at times, would be a conflict as neither trusted or liked the other.

An article, originally written by Grace Bjork, in the Greeley County Republican, Museum Chatter Section states:[60]

"1923, Raymond Estes moved to the C.S. Hurt Ranch on the White Woman Creek in Greeley County. Downstream from the ranch house was a natural spring-fed pond known as the Jumbo. In early days, a settler had built a large (jumbo) paddle wheel about four feet across, this was set in the creek bed and a shallow well dug—the wheel was set so that it only caught the north and south winds—as it was never shut off, the excess water gathered in the shallows below. Livestock watering would enlarge the pond, thus insuring a larger supply of water. When spring rains fell, the flooded creek would enlarge the pond even more. Over the years, the jumbo wheel was washed away and the floods enlarged the "Watering Hole" until it was washed down to the water level and to a spring that kept it filled during the years of drought. In the 1930's, the pond was large enough to accommodate a swimming party of 50 or more. How many of the then young people around Horace remember their Sunday School teachers, Jimmy and Edna Dizmang, bringing them out to the Boxelder grove and a swim in the Jumbo afterwards?

"On the north bank of the creek and upstream from the jumbo was, according to legend, a grave of a white woman killed by the Indians. Thus, the origin of the name White Woman Creek. By the grave was planted a wild rose and although the grave was never marked, the wild roses have spread over the entire creek bank, a living memorial of love for one of the many pioneers who crossed the barren prairie of Western Kansas."

Additionally, there are two articles in the Horace Greeley Museum section of the Greeley County Republican pertaining to a 4th of July celebration that Tribune was having. They state, "See the old Government Barrel Springs where the Beautiful White Woman was massacred by the Indians at Barrel Spring July 4th, 1888.[61][62][63] And this is also in Sarah Raymond's book, "Crossing The Plains," and is further explained in Chapter X.

This could be the solution to the question, "Why is the White

Woman Creek so named?" Unfortunately, it can't be proven and there is no written record of it, the grave was never marked, and there is no other evidence to prove the grave ever existed. It's all hearsay and just adds to the puzzle.

I remember when we would have a heavy rain storm in Tribune we would all rush down to the creek and watch to see how high the creek water would come up. You could almost tell how much rain we got by how high the water level in the creek was. I've seen it come up and almost go over the bridge, which is probably about 40 feet above the creek bed. The water at that level would be a fast flowing and dangerous torrent of water. It would take anything downstream that got in its way.

I also remember that when the creek was dry, it had a sandy creek bed and was hard to walk on. One year my friend, Robert Folsom, had just acquired a quarter horse which his dad, Archie, had gotten it for him. The horse was unbroken yet though. So Archie, Robert, and I led the horse to the creek from the Folsom house in Tribune and then Archie and Robert took turns making the horse walk in circles in the soft sand to wear him out. It worked. After a while, Robert walked up to the horse, threw a blanket on it, and got on. The horse did a few half-hearted bucks and then started walking again. It was broken-in. Archie's plan of walking the horse worked.

One time when several of us boys were out walking in the creek bed just west of the bridge about a mile, we found some old bones in the bank of the creek. They were buried about four feet down from the top of the ground on the bank. I guess they were uncovered by the erosion caused by the creek's running water. We were excited. Of course we let our imaginations run wild.

It could be anything, we thought. From Indian bones, to wild animal, maybe another mastodon, to buffalo bones, or to just ordinary cow bones. We, in all our wisdom, determined it was just cow bones. Who knows? I would like to go back to that place and look again. Someday soon, maybe I will.

Recently published (Oct 11, 2017) in the Greeley County Republican, Horace Greeley Museum Section, is a little blurb about an incident that occurred on June 1, 1906 regarding some human bones that were found. The article states:[64]

"01—June—1906—The skeleton of a man, woman, and child were found in the north part of Wichita County last week, where they had been buried near a bank which caved off and exposed the bones. There is considerable speculation as to who they were. The skull of the man indicated that he had been killed by a blow on the head. It is recalled that a family by the name of Albright disappeared from that part of the countY in the early days, about twenty years ago, but it was thought they had just left the country. It is not likely any further information will ever be known of the murders, if that was what it was."

As mentioned earlier, Kansas was going through a "bloody time" in the 1860s. The skeletons found in the bank of, I'm assuming a creek bed and wondering if it was White Woman Creek, in 1868 may have been the result of some pro-slavery hooligans that were causing havoc in Kansas during this period. On the other hand, they may have been killed by ordinary criminals taking advantage of a helpless family on the open prairie. This seems more likely. I don't believe the Indians killed them because they were not scalped and they were apparently buried. Indians would have killed and scalped them and would not have buried them. An ordinary criminal would have taken the time to bury them and conceal their deaths. As the article states, it is not likely we will ever know.

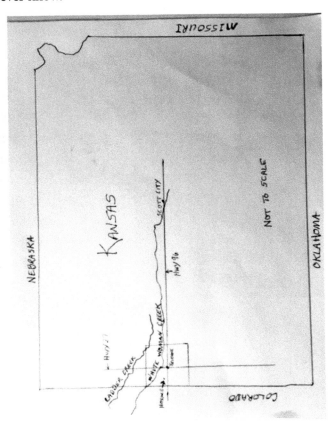

Map Showing Tribune, Kansas and White Woman Creek

4. THE BIKE TREK/BRIDGE

GOD ALMIGHTY WHAT FUN AND FREEDOM WE HAD AS YOUNG boys growing up in Western Kansas during the 1950's. We were allowed to do things back then that would be totally forbidden now by a host of people, number one, our parents. My have things changed!

In the summer of 1954, I was 11 years old. Later, in the month of August, I would turn 12. I remember several of us boys were almost always together doing things only boys back then would be doing. One time there were four of us and we planned on riding our bikes on the highway (Route 27) north out of our town (Tribune) to an intersection known as the "13 Mile Road Intersection». That's because it was supposedly exactly 13 miles north of Tribune. At the intersection, just off the highway to the northwest stood an old dilapidated, rundown and abandoned farmhouse, a small barn and a corral for horses. The highway was mostly straight and flat, although it had a couple of fairly steep hills to navigate for young boys on some old run-down Schwinn bikes. We didn't have all the fancy gear shifting, small tires, and light weight the bikes of today have. But they were hardy bikes with one gear. We went everywhere on them. Why walk when you can ride your bike? We planned and planned the trip. How far was it, how long would it take us to peddle it, how hot would it be, what should we take to drink and eat and what did we have to take our food in and what should we wear.

Hats or some kind of head covering was extremely important to us because of the hot summer sun. If we didn't have a hat, we decided we would take off our tee shirts and wrap them around our heads. We even considered what we would do if one of us got a flat tire or some other kind of mechanical problem like a chain breaking. We knew we could always leave the bike and have our dads take us back to get it in the next day or two. Basically, we decided we would ditch the bike and ride double. For sure none of us wanted to ride double so we checked our bikes as best we could, made sure there was ample air in the tires, the seat was adjusted correctly, and the chain was tight and lubed.

We told our parents what we were doing and to our surprise they just said, "Be careful, watch out for cars on the highway." I was a little shocked my mother didn't raise more of a fit about us going but it sort of reassured me that we would make the trek and come out okay. I was excited about going on our little adventure. I know it doesn't sound like much, but to us, 13 miles was a long, long ways on those old bikes and then we had to peddle another 13 miles back to Tribune. 26 miles. Wow!

The day finally came. It was a hot, hot August day in Kansas. I remember the joy I had when we finally started out. It was about 08:30 in the morning and the sun wasn't at its hottest yet. I had a plastic container of water and a peanut butter and jelly sandwich I strapped to the cross bar on my bike. I was ready and rearing to go.

Pat Grubb and Errol Woolen were the oldest of us. They were one year older than Dan Epp and I and they took the lead. I think the whole adventure was Pat's idea. He was always coming up with something! Today it was the bike trek. It all started out great because right out of the city limits there was a hill going downhill to the White Woman Creek bridge that was about 1/2 mile north of town. We had all heard that the bridge had been named for some white woman that had been killed by Indians. None of us knew what the real story behind it was, nor did we, at that time, care.

We coasted and then pedaled a little due to our excitement. The breeze in our faces and the speed we were going was sheer exuberance. Then we crossed the bridge and started up the other side, which was 3/4 of a mile uphill. It then became abundantly clear that this was going to be work. As we pedaled we laughed and talked about how much "fun" this was as we went. It soon set in how much work this was going to be and we shortly stopped talking and laughing as much and settled into the grueling work it was fast becoming.

At around 1:00 in the afternoon we arrived at the 13-mile intersection. The dirt road leading to the west from the intersection led to my uncle's house, which was another 10 miles or so. My family used to load up in Dad's old Packard and we'd go to my Aunt and Uncle's (the Konecne's) farm house and have a big Sunday dinner. They had a large family, seven boys and two girls, and so all the kids would play games like "kick-the-can" when it got dark. The men would smoke cigars and play poker, and the women would initially fix dinner and then clean up the dining room and kitchen and then gossip. We often would have homemade ice cream, which was wonderful. The kids took turns adding ice and salt to the ice cream machine and cranking the handle until the ice cream was made. Everyone had a great time. We did this mostly only during the summer months because the roads were almost impassable during the winter months and all the kids had school and homework to do. As we made the turn at the 13-mile intersection and headed back toward Tribune, I thought of my Konecne cousins and the good times we had there.

Once we made the turn and headed home we were like a bunch of horses going to water. We regained our energy level and it seemed like most of the way back was on a slight downhill. We stopped and ate our sandwiches in the ditch by the road and then started home again. Pat then yelled a kind of Indian or Rebel yell and rode his bike off the highway through a ditch and directly into a wheat field that had not been harvested yet. The wheat stalks were about four feet high. Of course the rest of us looked at each other as if to ask, "What was Pat doing now?" We then shrugged our shoulders as if to say, "What the hell", and then we all yelled and followed Pat into the wheat field. The wheat stalks were green and it seemed cool to us laying down. We laid the bikes down and just lay there for a while cooling off and regaining our strength. We were worried that the owner of the wheat field had, or would, see us and we would get in trouble for damaging some of his wheat. So we kept an eye out for traffic on the highway that would slow down when they neared us. We would have been hard to see in the wheat field but our tracks and the trail of damaged wheat stalks would have given us away. I don't know what we would have done if anyone did slow down.

Fortunately, no one did. There was little traffic on the roadway. We were soon back on the highway and pedaling for home.

My legs were tired and my butt was sore. I definitely was not used to riding this far in one fell swoop. It turned out I was not alone. All of us felt the same way, but we were back to laughing and talking a lot after having rested and drinking some of our water. On the way back we decided we would stop at the White Woman bridge and investigate it.

We arrived at the bridge in good time. Once you see your objective in the distance and know you can stop doing what you are doing, you speed up in order to get there faster to stop the pain you are currently feeling. We rode our bikes off the side of the road and took a path that led directly under the bridge. According to UglyBridges.com, whose source of information is the National Bridge Inventory (and it says the information is not verified. Use at your own risk) the White Woman Bridge is 65' long, 25.9' width between curbs, main spans material is concrete, and it was built in 1957.[65] I believe it's now constructed of concrete and steel with an asphalt 2-lane road on top. It's been there like that as long as I can remember. An article in the Greeley County Republican dated 28 June 2017 states, "Aug. 5, 1915—The cement bridge across the White Woman north of town was completed yesterday."[66] Another article in the Greeley County Republican states that on 1 April 1886, "Our men have been fixing a crossing of the White Women."[67] I'm not sure what this means. As stated it could mean a farmer is simple constructing a bridge of some type on his farm in order to cross the creek. It could mean the bridge that is just north of Tribune.

Under the bridge the local boys and girls displayed their artistic talents and expressed their views on one subject or another. Mostly it was sexually oriented. Some of it was pornographic. There were rough drawings of couples making love, hearts with arrows through them and initials in them of who loves who. There were dirty poems and drawings of male and female genitalia. I don't have any idea who actually got under the bridge and did all this but whoever it was they certainly had to be somewhat acrobatic because the beams and other areas where the graffiti was drawn was high and in a lot of extremely hard to get to places. Most of the graffiti was done in paint by a brush, but some was done using chalk. To us young boys it was about things we knew nothing about personally…yet, but were highly interested in at the time.

White Woman Creek Bridge. Photo by Robert Peterson

White Woman Creek Bridge. Photo by Robert Peterson

We finally left the bridge and headed uphill toward Tribune and home. We arrived home about 6:00 pm, just in time for supper. What a day!!

In July 2017, I was traveling through Kansas and my hometown of Tribune. I decided to go to the White Woman Creek bridge and take pictures of the graffiti there. Much to my dismay, the bridge has been updated and improved. I don't know when it was updated but now it did not have any drawings or graffiti on it at all. The creek bed was dry, but there was an overgrowth of weeds etc. in it now. Even the creek bed didn't look the same. What a disappointment. All things change, I guess. But sometimes it's hard to let go of those memories. I took a picture of the bridge, (See Figures above of the White Woman Bridge). In the picture, you can see the city of Tribune in the background. When I took the picture, I thought of when we were teenagers and drag raced our or our daddy's car across the bridge. Even that

73

seemed like it had changed drastically. Gone was the old asphalt and black skid marks from the tires. It just seemed "different" in so many ways. Aaahhh those memories!

5. THE CAMPSITE/GHOST

THAT SAME SUMMER THE FOUR OF US BOYS, PAT, ERROL, DAN, and I, plus Robert Folsom, would explore Tribune's local trash dump, which was just north of Tribune and just a short distance to the east from the highway and White Woman Creek bridge. The trash dump was basically in and on the sides of the White Woman Creek bed. To get to it one had to take a narrow dirt road and travel about 1/2 mile east of the bridge. There was a small house where one would leave the highway and take the dirt road leading to the trash dump. I think whoever lived there kept watch over the trash dump. We never saw him nor did we worry about him because we were just five young boys going to the trash dump. What harm could we do?

We would go there searching for nothing in general, but always hoping we would find something worth our efforts. During a heavy rain, some of the material in the dump would wash away downstream. As with most trash dumps, the stuff in it is 99 per cent garbage. However, to five young boys, a lot of it is priceless. We would find something and then if it wasn't destroyed already we'd destroy it by throwing things at it, kicking it, hitting it with something such as rocks or wooden sticks. Sometimes we would find something that we thought was worth something and carry it around until its usefulness wore out. It was still interesting.

Almost always we would see rats, snakes, spiders, ground squirrels, etc. It was never dull to go to the dump with your friends. Every now and then we would bring one of our dad's .22 cal. rifles and shoot up things. We didn't do it very often for fear of getting into trouble. Besides, most of the time the rats didn't come out until after dark and we would be long gone by then. But the biggest deterrent to us bringing a rifle was money. It cost money to buy bullets, even if they were only .22 cal. rounds, they still cost money and we for sure didn't have any.

One day while we were exploring the creek, which was dry at the time, and the dump, we came across an area in the creek bank that had been carved/chiseled out by the creek water when the water was up. The area was approximately 50 feet long and 20 feet wide. It was relatively flat and abutted a tall embankment of about 15 feet. It was perfect for us. It put us on flat ground and out of the wind which always blows in Kansas.

We decided right off the bat to play cowboys and Indians. Pat remembers seeing a trunk full of neckties in a trunk in the trash dump. He got them and handed them out. We tied them around our heads, using them as head bands and letting them dangle to one side or the other of our heads. We used them as belts as well to put our pretend tomahawks in. Somebody found some feathers from a dead hawk and so we put one or two of them in our hair. They were held in place by the tie we had tied around our head. It would have been difficult to act as a cowboy since we didn't have any cowboy items. So, we took our shirts off and painted our faces and chests with a little mud from the creek and some grease and oil from old auto parts in the junkyard. We thought we needed to do more to really play the part of an Indian.

There was a stand of cattail and tall strong reeds of some type in and next to the dry creek bed. We cut and gathered up several tall (approximately 6 or 7 feet) ones and used them as poles for the foundation for our, soon to be, teepees. We used some of the ties we had found and anything else we could find to tie one end of the poles together. Once tied, we stood them up and spread them out at the bottom. It was our teepee framework. It was great! We then covered the poles on the outside using anything we could find. We used cloth from the dump, some tumbleweeds and prairie grass. Once covered they actually looked pretty good to us. They fit the bill as our teepees anyway. They were small but for our purposes they were great. Each one of us had his own teepee. It was sort of a battle as to who got the best spots on the ground and the best cloth to cover the poles, but we finally ironed it all out and the teepees were erected.

Next, we made a circle of small rocks in front of each teepee so we could build a fire in front of them. We gathered dried grass and a few pieces of wood from the dump for the fires. We were in business. Each of us lit and built a small fire in front of "his" teepee. We talked a lot about how the Indians communicated with each other using fires. For example, one puff of smoke would mean something like, "We see the enemy", two puffs would mean, "The enemy was headed our way", etc. We also dug a small trench around the base of our teepees just in case it rained, which in all probability it wouldn't have.

We had a couple of pocket knives so we fashioned a couple of spears using the cattails and tried to make a bow with some wood we found. That fizzled out. The wood was no good and we didn't know what we were doing. We had to settle for spears and a couple of pocket knives.

One of the big discussions was who were we and what were we to call ourselves. Since we were now Indians, we needed a name for our little band of Indians and we had to have a name for each of us. The only Indian names we could think of were names like Geronimo, Cochiese, Sitting Bull, etc. We argued for a while as to who would get what name and in the end we couldn't decide on names. So, we decided that when we came back the next day we would have selected a name for ourselves and have a recommended name for our "band of Indians".

Time was one of our main concerns. We all had to be home by dark. Staying there after dark just wasn't feasible. Number 1, our parents would kill us if we stayed there after the sun went down. In those days, a kid could do pretty much anything in our small town during the day but their butt better be home before the sun went down to be in time for supper. Number 2, we didn't want to stay there too late. Fear of the dark, fear of our parents, and most importantly, fear of missing supper. Beside we knew we could come back the next day and have even more "Indian items" and things to do. We took a vote and decided what time to head back to town in order to be home on time. We decided 5:00 pm would work. It would take us about an hour to walk back to town.

It was coming up on 5:00 pm when all of us heard and saw her/it. We first heard a low wailing voice coming from the creek near the dump and when we looked toward the sound of the wailing, we saw a misty/cloud like shape moving away from us in the dry creek bed. We all looked at each other with a "what the shit is that" kind of look on all our faces. When we looked back, it was still there and the wailing wasn't getting any louder but was getting plainer to hear. It sounded like a woman wailing over the loss of a loved one. It made the hair on our necks stand up and goose bumps on our arms form. We just stood there and quietly watched the mist move and listened to the wailing for about four minutes. None of us said a word. It was a surreal moment. It actually scared the devil out of us. We didn't know what it was but it was definitely there and making a wailing sound. It couldn't have been the wind whistling through some of the trash piles in the dump because there wasn't any wind. It was a perfectly quiet and peaceful evening up until that point. Just as suddenly as it appeared, it disappeared and we heard no more wailing.

The Ghost Of White Woman Creek

We all spoke at once saying, "Let's get the hell outta here" and started picking up some of our things so we could head home. We then immediately headed home because we didn't want to stay there any longer. We were half walking and half running. Our excuse was it's getting late and we've got to be home on time. In actuality, it scared us so bad none of us wanted to stay there any longer. Nor did we go in the direction that we had come. That would have meant that we would have to walk in the creek bed where we saw the "mist" and go through the trash dump to reach the highway and then head for home. No, we automatically started home by cutting across country. We took a straight line toward Tribune and home. We went through fields and had to cross barbed wire fences, but it didn't matter. We weren't going in the creek bed.

On the way home, we remained silent till we were about half-way home. Then we all started talking about what we thought we had just seen and heard. Someone mentioned the wind and the rest of us immediately ruled that out because of no wind. Someone mentioned gases escaping from the dump and we ruled that out because we thought a gas might cause the mist but not the wailing. We were stumped as to what we saw and heard. Errol mentioned that someone might be playing a trick on us by using a recording of the wailing and putting it on a speaker. He said his older brother, Bill, would be just the one to do such a thing. We all ruled that out because Bill was currently out of town and besides he didn't know where we were and we would have seen him coming.

Pat said, "It had to be the ghost of the white woman that was killed by the Indians. That's why the creek is named White

Woman Creek. Didn't you guys know that?" No one said anything at first but we were all thinking he was right. We had all
heard that the reason the creek was so named was because years
ago a white woman was killed by the Indians, but we had all
heard several different versions of what exactly happened. To
counter Pat's theory, we then said if it was a ghost, what the devil
was it doing in the creek by the trash dump. Such an odd place.
No one had an explanation.

And no one knew the full/true story behind the creek's name.
But I knew I, and probably the rest of the guys, would ask their
parents or someone about the history of White Woman Creek
when we got home.

It was a little after 6:00 pm when I got home. I was safe. It
wasn't dark yet and mom was just setting the table for supper. I
had made it in time. I was relieved I made it on time. No one was
angry at me and supper was ready. Couldn't get any better. Plus,
I was starved. When I walked into the kitchen to tell mom I was
home, she took one look at me and said, "What have you been
into?"

I had forgotten that I still had mud and oil on my face and
arms. I looked a mess. I told her that we had been playing Indians in White Woman Creek down by the trash dump and put
mud and oil on ourselves to play the part. She merely smiled and
quickly said, "Okay, clean up real quick, daddy's home and supper
is ready." At the dinner table mom told dad, who also had just
gotten home, that I had been out playing Indians all day down by
the trash dump in the creek.

For fear of getting into trouble or being looked at like I was
a crazy person, I decided to wait and tell someone what we had

seen at the trash dump. For sure I wasn't going to ask dad. Mother was the best bet and I decided I'd wait until morning before I asked her. Mothers were always more understanding than fathers when it came to asking about weird or eerie things. I used to ask mom about what my nightmares and other things meant and was always listened to and never laughed at. I knew mom was my go-to person.

In any case, I knew I had to find out more about the mist we saw. But as soon as mom told dad what we had been doing and where we were, he nonchalantly said, "You see the ghost"? I was shocked, to say the least.

"How did he know?" I thought. So I asked him, "How did you know, dad?" He said he could tell by my demeanor that I had something up my sleeve and wanted to talk to somebody about it so he just guessed about the ghost. He hit the nail on the head! I had to know more and when supper was over I asked him if he would tell me what he knew about the "ghost" that appears in the White Woman Creek area.

My father proceeded to fill up one of his pipes so he could have his "after-supper" and work smoke. I always liked the aroma of his pipes. And after supper the family during the summer time, when there wasn't any school work to do or any pressing task that had to be done, tended to sit around the table and talk about the events of the day. Bear in mind, we didn't have TV's in those days, so unless we had something pressing to do, we sat at the kitchen table for a while and just talked. I loved it.

Mom would talk about our relatives, the groceries, the garden, things that needed fixed around the house like the washing machine or water-cooled air conditioner. Dad generally talked about his gasoline business (he was the local Standard Oil Distributor), the weather, the problems with his gasoline routes, his "coyote-wagon" (which was an old Plymouth that he had chopped off everything behind the front seat and put roll-bars in it). He "souped" it up and would take it coyote hunting once or twice a month. Not only did he enjoy it, he got $2.00 for each coyote ear he turned in to the county. Some of the local farmers would also hang the coyotes they shot up by their rear legs on fence posts that ran parallel to the main highways. On the highway near Syracuse, Kansas (a town 34 miles south of Tribune) the string of coyotes on fence posts ran for close to a mile. Dad was an avid hunter. He always had a lot of shotguns, rifles, and ammunition stacked in the upstairs closet. He always told us kids to stay away from them because they were always loaded. We took him at his word. I don't remember ever touching them unless he was there to supervise me.

My older sister, Janice, would help mom with the dishes and mostly talked about girl things with mom, what the latest fad or fashion in clothes was and getting her driver's license. My two younger sisters, Linda and Barbara, didn't have much to say at the table. They were too young. They just wanted down from the table so they could get out their coloring books or dolls and go play.

Dad, at last, looked at me and said that he would tell me what he knew about the ghost. He said that he didn't know if any of what he knew was true or not because it was only what he had heard from some of the locals talking about it. He, himself, didn't believe in ghosts, spirits walking the earth, or anything like that. His beliefs were reinforced because he had never seen a ghost or spirit and, consequently, thought it was all a bunch of old wives' tales, a bunch of malarkey, and a bunch of gobble-d gook. Never-the-less, he said he would talk to me about it to quell my anxie-ties.

As it turned out, dad didn't know much about the history of the ghost. He simply said that years ago a white woman was captured by some Indians. He said the Army had sent some sol-diers here to get her back and when they found the Indians and the white woman a battle ensued and she was killed. Reportedly, she has since roamed the White Woman Creek area as a ghost. He said that several people have reported seeing and hearing her moan, but he didn't believe them. He said people also believe in UFO's, Santa Claus, the tooth fairy, leprechauns, the abdominal snowman, bigfoot, and a host of other silly things. He said our minds were playing tricks on us and that I shouldn't worry about it.

Not that dad was a constant church-goer, he was religious, believing in Jesus Christ. We were Lutherans and I think that dad just didn't believe in spirits or ghosts based on his personal religious beliefs. I was determined though to find out more about ghosts, especially the one we saw. I couldn't wait to meet up with my friends to see what they had learned about it.

As it turned out, none of my friends spoke of our little inci-dent with their parents. A couple of them mentioned it to their older siblings and when they were laughed at, they just dropped the subject and stopped inquiring about it.

For whatever reason or reasons, we never went back. Perhaps it was because we were afraid of what we'd find or because we were afraid of what everyone would be saying about those cra-zy boys thinking they saw and heard a ghost in the creek. Or, perhaps we didn't go back because we all had different things going on and time and availability didn't match up for us all to go there at once. I, for one, for example was not about to go there by myself. No way! Now that I'm older and not afraid of the boogie man anymore, I would like to go back to the same old spot and sit and listen and perhaps see and/or hear the "ghost" again. However, I doubt that will ever happen due to my living so far away now and having far too many other priorities. I, and my friends that were there, are just going to have to chalk it up as one of those childhood experiences we shared. We know what we saw and heard, whether anyone else believes us or not is moot. We don't care.

6. THE MANY LEGENDS

IT WASN'T UNTIL YEARS LATER WHEN I READ AN ARTICLE IN the "History of Early Greeley County" that peeked my interest again in the legend about the ghost of White Woman Creek.

The article was titled "Legend of White Woman Creek", which is excerpts from a story by Chick Reid (compiled by Daniel Brown) and states that the creek is a "stand-alone" creek, meaning that it does not start from any other stream or water source and it does not empty into any other stream. It goes on to say that there is plenty of evidence that at one time the creek was a "beautiful, clear running stream". It also says, "History relates that in the year 1869 Indian raiders captured two white women at the Spillman Creek massacre in Lincoln Co., Ks.[68] and that some two years later U.S. troops rescued one of them in a demented condition in Western Kansas. A Mr. Moore, who used to live in Great Bend enjoyed telling of the rescue by his cavalry troop, of a crazy white woman who wanted to stay with the Indians instead of going back to the white settlements. He placed the action in Greeley Co. near old Barrel Springs and Wild Horse Coral. Others have placed it further east, either in Wichita or Scott County."

The article then goes on to tell the story of the Legend of

White Woman Creek. I did not speak to, or correspond with, the author of the story. To me the title tells it all ... It's a LEGEND. However, it is such a great story that, for fear of changing it, I will relate it as written. It is as follows:

"Many, many moons ago, water flowed freely between the banks of this stream. Great herds of bison and antelope roamed these prairies and the Cheyenne nation hunted here unmolested.

One hunting season a young Cheyenne chieftain, Tee-Wah-Nee led a small party of braves across the prairies in the annual hunt. Many hides and a great store of meat they accumulated by the time they camped near the bank of the River-that runs-between-the-hills-that-are-always-covered-with-smoke. They camped for many days to cure the meat and treat the hides.

One night a band of white settlers attacked and plundered the camp, ran off many horses, stole much meat and many hides and rode away to their home settlement. Many of the braves had been wounded, among them, Chief Tee-Wah-Nee and his brother Tan-Ka-Wah. A band of braves followed the trail of the white men, took ten of them prisoner, and took two white women from the settlement.

They made the white men carry back to the hunting camp all the stolen meat and robes, and put them at the tasks of caring for the camp. In Indian custom, this is the work of the women, so the braves constantly taunted the white men as squaw-workers. The two girls were set to work caring for the braves wounded in the raid.

During the three moons while Anna-Wee and her sister May-O-Wee cared for and nursed the chieftain and his followers back to health, it became evident to all the hunting party that Chief Tee-Wah-Nee and his brother Tan-Ka-Wah had fallen in love with their white nurses, and that their love was returned by the girls.

When the day had been set for breaking camp and starting the homeward journey, the assembled braves gave their consent and the Chieftain at once proclaimed himself to be the husband of Anna-Wee and his brother to be the husband May-O-Wee.

It was unusual for women to speak at a council meeting but Anna-Wee signified that she wished to speak to the assembly. Acclamation indicated that the braves were glad to give her the right to speak to them.

Having learned the Cheyenne tongue, while attending the task of nursing, she told them it was the custom of her people, the pale faces, for a husband to make a gift to the bride at their marriage. She asked as a gift that after the hunting party had made five days' journey towards its home village, the white men be released to return to their own settlement, provided they gave their word of honor never to steal again from the red man and never to try to take the girls away from their husband's people and return them to the white settlement. "You know, our only brother is among those you hold, and we are thinking of him and his future happiness in making this request," she said.

The braves held council, and decided to grant the request, if the white men should agree. However, Anna-Wee's brother,

89

speaking for the white men, said none of the prisoners desired to return to the settlement where they had lived, as they had no families there and felt they would not be able to get the settlers to respect any oath they might take. He asked that they be allowed to remain with the tribe, not as captives, but as adopted brothers. The braves immediately granted this request.

Scouts rode ahead of the party and the home village was thus fully informed of the happening with highly complementary tales of the gentleness, skillfulness and wisdom of the brides. The arrival was a gala event, as all the colorful magnificence of tribal regalia and all the dignity and splendor of an Indian ceremonial feast of Thanksgiving was in progress to welcome the hunters and newcomers into the arms of the tribe.

Some twenty moons passed and the Cheyenne were again at their annual hunting grounds. The happiest lodge in the entire village was that of Chief Tee-Wah-Nee and Anna-Wee. They were the proud parents of a son, just beginning to crawl when allowed out of his papoose basket. The two winters had been mild and the summers fruitful for the tribe and all seemed well, when word came that one of the adopted white men called Henrich had deserted the tribe and started on his way back to the white settlements.

No effort was made to overtake Henrich and return him to the tribe, although in going he had stolen one of the chief's finest ponies.

After several skirmishes with cavalry troops it was learned that Henrich had told the troops from Fort Wallace that the white men and women with the Cheyennes were still prisoners and were being mistreated. Chief Tee-Wah-Nee planned to send several of the white boys to the fort to tell the truth, however, before the arrangements could be completed, Henrich persuaded the troops to attack the Cheyenne village, even though some of the officers and many of the troops hesitated because when they had encountered the hunting parties, none of the whites had attempted to come to them.

Near the end of the first day's fighting, Chief Tee-Wah-Nee met his death at the hand of Henrich, the traitor. After the chieftain fell, Henrich rode to the lodge of Anna-Wee, overpowered her, murdered her son and, taking her on his horse, rode away down the stream now known as the White Woman Creek. A short distance away from the scene of the battle, the grief-stricken girl craftily played faint, and as they neared the body of the fallen brave, she asked her captor to let her rest awhile.

In a few moments, she went to the body of the brave, pretending to seek ornaments from it, but soon faced her captor armed with the bow and arrows of the dead one. Swiftly she shot an arrow into Henrich's chest. Then as he lay dying she cried, "You are a traitor to both your own people and my adopted people. You have this day brought trouble and suffering to all mankind."

She took his rifle and ammunition, together with the bow and arrows, and returned to the battle scene, where every bullet she fired and every arrow she shot accounted for a horse or a soldier. As darkness descended, Anna-Wee eluded the troops and with the help of others from the village, carried the body of the chieftain husband to the ruins of their lodge. She spent the night beside the remains of her husband and son, singing death chants of the Cheyenne and imploring Manitou, the great spirit of the red man, to take their spirits to the Happy Hunting Ground for an eternity of peace and pleasure.

Anna-Wee went out with the braves to fight against the second day's assault on the village. As evening brought an end to this days fighting, Anna-Wee fell, mortally wounded. As night spread its mantle of darkness over the scene of destruction and resolution, she made her last plea to the great spirit of her adopted people: "Oh Manitou, be kind to my chieftain husband and to my little son. Forgive me the love I bore for them, which has been the cause of this conflict, and let me join them in the Happy Hunting Ground that our spirits may always abide together in the peace and contentment there. In some way let the lesson of this day teach the white men that the Indian only fights for the home and the hunting grounds that are his by the right of heritage, and thus bring about better understanding between our races."

It does not require a very vivid imagination when one sits on the banks of the stream bed on a spring evening to see in the mists that arise from the sands the spirit of Anna-Wee as she wanders among the scenes of her happiness, and-if you listen carefully, you can still hear Anna-Wee's gentle voice in her plea to Manitou, the great spirit of her husband's people, pleading that the day may be hastened when there will be a better understanding between the White man and the Indian.

Once you have seen her there and heard her plea, there will nevermore be doubt in your mind as to why this stream bed is known as, "White Woman Creek."[69]

I also learned of another story about the ghost of White Woman Creek that was published in "Legends of Kansas, History, Tales, and Destinations in the Land of Kansas, The Ghost of White Woman Creek". In this article, it states there are several versions of how the creek got its name. The first tells of a Cheyenne Indian attack in the late 1800's. The Cheyenne were said to have attacked a western settlement in retaliation for an earlier raid on their camp by white men. After several white men were killed, the Indians recaptured their stolen goods, and kidnapped 12 white settlers—10 men and two women. As time passed, the two white women decided to stay with the tribe and married Cheyenne men. One of the women, who the Indians called Ann-Wee, fell in love with Chief Tee-Wah-Nee, and bore him a son. Most of the white men were accepted and remained with the Cheyenne. However, there was one man who was eager to leave. After many months with the tribes, he was able to steal a horse and made his way to Fort Wallace in present-day Wallace County, KS. Upon his arrival, he convinced the army that the remaining whites were being held against their will. The escaped man led a group of soldiers to the Indian camp and the soldiers attacked, killing the Chief and his infant son. As the battle continued, his wife, Anna-Wee retaliated by killing the man who had betrayed them. She then continued to defend the tribal village she had come to think of as home, and in the end, she too, was slain.[70]

It also says, "Another story tells of an Indian war party that was raiding homesteads in the area in the 1870's. During the raid, they also attacked an Army ambulance, they tortured and killed the soldiers and kidnapped a woman who was traveling with the ambulance. The warriors rode off with the woman and one night while camping along a creek, she was able to escape. One version of the tale says that in order to avoid the same tortures she had seen inflicted upon the ambulance driver, she stole a rope from the Indians while they camped, ran to a tree on the banks of the creek and hanged herself before her captors could stop her. Another version says that the last that the Indians saw of her, she was running up a dry stream bed, and it is believed she perished on the prairies." Since the late 1800's, legend has it that on moonlight nights the specter of a woman has often been seen running along the old stream bed. Others have heard her singing a mournful Indian song.[71]

Another article on the story is available by going to "Historical Site (http://www.lasr.net/travel/KS+tribune+historical-sites&travelTl=KS100702). That's a mouthful that brings up the legend again on the internet. It basically just states the same story as that of Anna-Wee above, but it does not mention names, dates, etc.[72]

An article in the Greenwood Encyclopedia of American Cultures states, "WPA Project workers reported rural legends such as the Greeley County ghost of White Woman Creek. This is a white-clad woman who drowned herself in the river when she found her lover lying dead on its banks."[73]

Additionally, the WPA Guide to Kansas, #34, The Sunflower State, had the same story as the Greenwood Encyclopedia.[74]

Also the story in the article printed in the Greeley County Republican newspaper, dated 29 June 2016 and written by Nadine Cheney that states the beautiful White Woman was massacred by the Indians at Barrel Springs July 4th, 1888.[75]

Legend has it that on moonlight nights, the specter of a woman has often been seen running along what is now a dry, creek bed, or that at other times, wandering slowly along the old stream bed. Others have heard her singing a mournful Indian song. Her singing an Indian song makes the last version of this version of the legend somewhat impossible because if she had just been captured, in 1868, and then rescued in six months later, she wouldn't have had time to learn the Indian language.

Two more interesting ghost stories about the ghost of White Woman Creek can be found on the "Seeks Ghosts" web site. The stories are similar to the ones above but says "one thing about White Woman Creek is not in doubt—this area is haunted."[76]

Another interesting version about the legend is told via a Hollywood movie for TV (See Chapter 7).

7. STOLEN WOMEN: CAPTURED HEARTS (THE MOVIE)

ONE OF THE BEST STORIES ABOUT THE LEGEND OF THE GHOST of White Woman Creek is told through a Hollywood made-for-television movie titled "Stolen Women: Captured Hearts." It was a 1997 made-for television film directed by Jerry London. [77] The film stars Janine Turner as Anna (Brewster) Morgan, a woman living on the plains of Kansas in 1868 who is kidnapped by a band of Lakota Indians. It also stars Patrick Bergin, Jean Louisa Kelly, Michael Greyeyes, and Rodney A. Grant. The story is loosely based on the real Anna (Brewster) Morgan who was taken by Lakota Indians for approximately one year before being returned to her husband. See Chapter VIII for the real story of Anna (Brewster) Morgan.

The movie story is set on the plains of Kansas in 1868, where General George Custer has destroyed a village of Cheyenne Indians. Seeking revenge, a band of Lakota Indians led by Tokalah (Michael Greyeyes) attack a wagon train headed to Fort Hays, Kansas, where they kill everyone in the wagons. However, strangely, when Tokalah comes to the last remaining wagon that is driven by Anna Brewster (Janine Turner), he finds her and one

97

of her friends, Sarah White, alive. He ends up letting her and her pregnant friend go.

Anna makes it to Fort Hays and is met by her brother Stewart (Ted Shackelford), a pastor, who has arranged for her to marry Daniel Morgan (Patrick Bergin). Not long after her "arranged" marriage, Anna is being visited by Sarah (Jean Louisa Kelly) when Tokalah and other Lakota Indians break into her home and take both women. Daniel and Stewart try to go after them, but are unsuccessful in following their trail, as is Captain Robert Farnsworth (Dennis Weaver) who later joins the hunt.

At the Lakota camp, Sarah resists blending in while Anna takes more readily to their culture as the months pass. She and Tokalah, who begins to learn English from young Cetan (Willam Lightning) who is half white from his soldier father, grow closer and Anna realizes she is falling in love with him. Not wanting to commit adultery, she decides to escape with Sarah and they steal horses one night. However, Tokalah and his warriors catch up with them. Tokalah sends the warriors back to their camp with Sarah. He and Anna stay. They argue, with Anna saying that she never asked to be taken from her husband, but Tokalah tells her that she did ask, claiming that he heard her. Giving into her feeling for him, they spend a passionate night together on the plains.

Back at Fort Hays, General Custer (Willam Shockley) arrives to take over the search using his favorite scout, a Native American named Bloody Knife. He, Farnsworth, Daniel and Stewart make contact with Tokalah and Chief Luta (Saginaw Grant) who tell him that they can have Sarah but not Anna. Daniel, her white husband, realizes that Tokalah has "lain with" Anna. Custer puts Luta under arrest, saying he will be hanged if both women are not returned. The next day, the Lakota return and a battle ensues, which ends poorly with a wounded Tokalah returning to camp. Soon after this, Sarah leaves and rides off to Custer's encampment. Anna tells Tokalah she must leave as well in order to spare Luta. Tokalah tells Anna that they belong together as he had seen her before in a vision, however, she still leaves to Custer's encampment and Luta is released.

Anna returns to her husband, Daniel, and their home. Sarah soon visits and tells Anna she must leave her husband as she (Anna) now knows where she belongs. After giving Daniel one last night together, Anna rides off to the Lakota camp only to find it destroyed. She then sees Tokalah still on the land, mourning. He assumes she is another vision, but she touches his face and confesses her love for him and they embrace.

That was the end of the movie.

8. SARAH WHITE AND ANNA BREWSTER MORGAN

THIS IS ANOTHER STORY ABOUT THE LEGEND OF WHITE Woman Creek that is very similar to the movie version but this one gives names, dates, places and can be researched. It's about Sarah White and Anna Brewster.

Sarah White was born December 10, 1850, at North Elk Grove, Wisconsin. She was one of seven children in the White family. The Whites moved and settled in Cloud County, Kansas, about eight miles west of present-day Concordia, Kansas. Their homestead was about five miles southwest of the Republican River on a small stream then known as Granny Creek. Because of what happened there the stream would later become known as White's Creek. On the morning of 13 August 1868, four Cheyenne warriors approached the homestead, entered the house and forced Mrs. White to cook them a meal. After they ate they ransacked the house. During the confusion, Mrs. White and Sarah's younger sisters escaped and hid in the brush by the nearby creek. The 17 year old Sarah, unfortunately, was captured and taken by the Indians. She was tied to a horse and after the four warriors and Sarah met up with 15 more Cheyenne warriors she was gang raped. The 15 other warriors had found Sarah's dad and brothers, who had been working in the fields. The Indians killed her dad. Her brothers escaped their attack. Sarah remembers the Indians as being Cheyenne Dog Soldiers.

Anna Brewster was born December 10, 1844, at New Brunswick, New Jersey. Her father, John W. Brewster, died four months before she was born. Consequently, the family lived in poverty. Her brother, Daniel A. Brewster, joined the 1st New Jersey, and her other brother (name unknown) joined the 7th New Jersey and they both fought in the Civil War. Daniel survived, however, the other brother died at Chancellorsville in 1863. After the war, Daniel moved his mother, Prudence Nau Brewster, and his sister, Anna, to Pennsylvania. His mother died there in an insane asylum. In 1867, Daniel and Anna moved to Kansas, on a 160-acre claim on the Solomon river in Ottawa County, near present day Delphos, Kansas.

Delphos is located 5 miles west of the I-35 and KS-41 intersection. Delphos was laid out as a town in 1869 by W. A. Kiser. It was officially recorded in January 1871. The name Delphos, was submitted by the first resident in this vicinity, Levi Yockey, who came from Delphos, Ohio. Like many Ohio towns, Delphos, Kansas was laid out around a square that became a tree-shaded green park with a bandstand near its center.

In September 1868, Anna, who was now 23 years old, married a James S. Morgan, who was 29 years old. James was also a Civil War veteran, having fought in the 2nd Colorado Cavalry. Anna and James moved into his dugout, which was two miles southwest from Delphos, near her brother Daniel's place.

Anna was said to be a very pretty young woman. She had blue

eyes and thick lustrous hair of yellow hue.[78] She was also a school teacher, according to an article on Anna Brewster's capture written and researched by Clayton L. Hogg, Chagrin Falls, OH. A synopsis of it is as follows:[79]

Anna Brewster Morgan was captured by Indians just northwest of present day Delphos, KS during a raid on October 3, 1868. Anna was a young, pretty, school teacher in Delphos and had been married less than a month to James Morgan. On that ill-fated day, Mr. Morgan was working in a field about a mile north of their dugout home when he was attacked by a band of Sioux Indians. (Note: In the book, "A Fate Worse Than Death," the authors say it was a band of Lakota Indians). They had just moved from their dugout home on the north side of the Solomon River to their new dugout on the south side of the river, about a half mile west of Delphos. When the Indians fired their rifles, it frightened his horses and they ran back to the dugout. Mrs. Morgan (Anna), saw the horses and, expecting the worst, strapped a pistol on her side, mounted one of the horses and set out to find her husband. Following the horses south, the Indians spied Anna approaching. They hid in the bushes, then pounced on her as she came up from the creek. They tied her to her horse and took her to their camp.

Anna's husband, James, had been shot in the hip but he survived the attack by limping off and hiding in a tall field of corn while the Indians went after the horses.

Later the Lakotas traded Anna to a band of Cheyenne Indians, who had earlier (13 August) kidnapped Sarah C. White near Concordia, KS. The two girls first met each other in the Cheyenne camp after the Lakota trade. During the more than five cold months of captivity and long travel they were doing, Anna and Sarah had given up all hope of a rescue. They planned, and executed, an escape but were soon recaptured and submitted to even more harsh treatment. Sarah kept resisting the Indians during her captivity. Anna, however, gave in to them because she thought she would not ever see another white person and because she thought she would not survive if she didn't. She ended up marrying a Cheyenne warrior and was then treated more kindly by the Indian women.

Anna's brother, Daniel, never stopped searching for Anna since her capture. He had linked up with the 19th Kansas Cavalry and then joined up with Custer's 7th Cavalry. He had told Gen. Custer that he required no horse, weapon, or pay, but only wished to search for his sister. Custer put him on the payroll as a substitute teamster. Later Gen. Custer would write that Brewster "displayed more genuine courage, perseverance, and physical endurance, and a greater degree of true brotherly love and devotion, than I have ever seen combined in one person."[80]

The two women, Sarah White and Anna Morgan, were finally rescued by Gen. George Custer on March 22, 1869. They were northwest of the Wichita Mountains near todays Lawton, Oklahoma. Custer had captured some Cheyenne and demanded the return of the two white women with the threat of hanging one of six chiefs being held hostage by Custer, each day. The Indians (Cheyenne Chief Stone Forehead) turned the two girls over to Custer as an exchange.

A few months after Anna's rescue, she gave birth to a half-Indian child. She named him Ira. Unfortunately, Ira died about two years later. Anna had three more children, but the unhappy marriage with Mr. Morgan ended when the youngest child was seven. Anna and her children moved in with her brother, Arthur Brewster, and lived with him until the children were grown. Then she finished her days in a small house in Delphos. She avoided publicity and was never accepted by the Delphos community after her capture. In her guilt-ridden, unhappy life she later admitted, "I often wished they had never found me." She was declared insane later and died at the age of 57 on June 11, 1902. She is buried not far from the entrance of the Delphos Cemetery, next to her son, Ira.

Mr. Hogg, the author of the article, goes on to say that he believes a cave, located four miles south and two and one-eighth miles east of Delphos that is carved out in a sandstone cliff, was used as a sacred "sweat lodge" for a Plains Indian tribe. It, reportedly, had several Indian petroglyphs but, unfortunately, the cliffs were now defaced with white man's names as well. The author's uncle, Mr. Floyd Hogg, had taken pictures of it in 1914. Scientists from one of the universities (the author didn't know which one) came and removed the petroglyphs. A few relics have been picked up in various sites around the area where old Indian villages were reported to have been located by the author and his father during the 1930's.

Additional information about Anna, James and their son, Ira, can be found by looking on the internet on the "Find A Grave" web site. It confirms the facts that there was a James S. Morgan and that he was wounded by the Indians that captured his wife in 1868. In 1900, he was living in Ottawa Co., KS. When Anna died in 1902, James moved to Mesa County, Colorado to be with his daughter, May "Maude" (Morgan) and her husband Murray

Townsend Carver. James died two years later, August 1904, in Delta County, Colorado and is buried in Mesa County, Colorado.[81]

The "Find A Grave" site on the internet also revealed/confirmed that Anna, whose real name was Amanda Belle "Anna" Brewster Morgan, was captured by the Indians and was their prisoner for six months; finally being rescued near the Washita Mountains by General Custer.[82]

Around 1901, Anna was taken to a mental asylum in Topeka, KS. The obituary states that Anna was working in the field alongside her husband when he was wounded and she was captured. She did not get on a horse that had "gone home" and then go to her husband. The obituary also states that James and Anna had four children, Ira Arthur Morgan, May Maud (Morgan) Carver, Claud Ralph Morgan, and B. Glendale Morgan. Anna died in the mental asylum on July 13, 1902, in Topeka, Shawnee County, KS.[83]

According to the "Find A Grave" web site her son, Ira, was most likely Indian as Anna had been a prisoner for six months, rescued in the spring of 1869 and Ira was born Dec. 3rd of that year. He died when he was 17 months old. He is buried in Ottawa County, KS.[84]

A pump in the field still marks their farm site.

Although the above is a great story about a female being captured / kidnapped by Indians and later rescued, in this case by Gen. George A. Custer at the Battle of Washita in November 1868, and there are grave markers in Kansas identifying the Morgan family with an attached obituary describing her ordeal, I don't believe she is the one the White Woman Creek was named after. First, she was rescued in Oklahoma territory. Not that it had to be in Kansas, but it makes more sense to name a local creek after something or someone that lived there locally. Although she lived in and was captured in Kansas, it was in eastern Kansas, not near Greeley County, Kansas where the creek is located. Secondly, Anna did not die until 1902. I believe if it had been her, someone, or some government official, would have brought her to the creek, identified her, named the creek after her and had a big celebration. This was not done. Therefore, I don't think it was her. Finally, Gen. Custer, being the egotist that he was, would have had something to do with the naming of the creek and the celebration. He would have, at the very least, sent a letter reminding everyone it was he that saved Anna. That way he would have received even more acclaim, which was his style.

9. THE COLDHART'S VERSION

THE COLDHARTS ARE KATIE HARTMAN AND NICK RYAN, TWO theater artists based in Brooklyn, New York. They create American Gothic-inspired music-theater. They travel to various theaters throughout the country performing. [85]

They have written a thirteen-song story about the ghost of White Woman Creek. [86] They are sung by Ms. Hartman. They have performed in Marienthal, KS. They later performed in Chicago and Orlando and still are performing in other parts of the country. The performance is basically Ms. Hartman playing a guitar and singing the songs about Anna Morgan Faber, who, according to the Coldharts, is the ghost of White Woman Creek. The songs are a chronological story of Anna Morgan Faber. Written below is what, I believe, is their version of the story. I'm basing it on the lyrics in the songs that Ms. Hartman sings and sells. [87]

Anna Morgan was a school teacher in West Virginia. She took a risk and left West Virginia to marry her brother's friend and comrade-in-arms, Heinrich Faber. They fought together on the Union side during the Civil War. Mr. Heinrich Faber, is a German-Catholic, who doesn't speak English very well and, according to Anna, is not very romantic. He now has a small, 160-

acre farm in Kansas. The year is 1867. Anna and Heinrich are living in a sod house and, although she is trying, she can't get pregnant. They are childless, which upsets Anna.

The farm they're working isn't producing much and they are struggling. One day Heinrich leaves with some friends and they raided a Cheyenne Indian village and took their meat and robes (bison skins). Shortly thereafter, some Indians broke into their farm house and took the meat and robes back. They also took Anna. Heinrich didn't put up much of a fight to prevent them from taking her.

Anna was terrified of being kidnapped by the Indians. She thought they would torture her and then kill her. However, when they arrived back at their camp they turned Anna over to a kindly old Indian squaw called "Little Thunder" and they worked together gathering wood and water and other small chores. Anna soon becomes unafraid and enjoys her new environment. She asks Little Thunder about one of the braves and is informed he is Chief an Tee-Wah-Nee and he is honorable in battle and that he's the "Man-Who-Makes-The-Crane-Come-When-He-Sings". Anna ends up marrying Chief Tee-Wah-Nee and the chief calls her Anna-Wee and they have a son, who they named Daniel.

Then one day the Cavalry came and attacked the village. Chief Tee-Wah-Nee was killed. Anna is rescued by the Cavalry and she and her son are taken back east to her husband, Heinrich. However, Heinrich doesn't like Daniel and after two years the people in the town still won't speak to her or Daniel. Heinrich says that because Daniel is a half-breed he can't even be baptized and should be drowned. Anna misses her Indian Chief husband, Chief Tee-Wah-Nee, and the Indian village.

Heinrich ends up drowning the baby Daniel and tells the town folk that Daniel died in his crib. Anna goes insane from the grief and she is locked up in a mental institution, where she dies. Anna's spirit then returns to walk the creek bed singing a hateful (she wants to kill all people that harmed her) and mournful song.

I don't know where Ms. Hartman got her information. I don't know where she came up with the names she was using or anything else. In the book "A Fate Worse Than Death" by Gregory and Susan Michno, it states that when Major Edward Wynkoop was trying to get the release of Mrs. Eubanks, Willie Eubanks, and Nancy Morton, one of the names of the Indian Chiefs he was dealing with was called "No-Ta-Nee".[88] This name is similar to the name the Coldharts were using (Chief Tee-Wah-Nee), but it was not the same. As they say, "Close, but no cigar."

Also Ms. Hartman states in her songs that she had a son by Chief Tee-Wah-Nee named Daniel. In the article, "Legend of White Woman Creek" in the book the History of Early Greeley County on page 97 it states that the female captured and the one who married the Chief was called "Anna-Wee" by the Indians and that after she married the Chief (Chief Tee-Wah-Nee) they had a son. It did not give his name. However, in the real capture of a Ms. Nancy Fletcher Morton on 8 August 1864 (See the next Chapter—The Nebraska Plum Creek and Oak Creek Massacres) there was also a young boy captured. His name was Danny Marble. The Indians thought young Danny Marble was Ms. Morton's son. It appears that's where Ms. Coldhart got the name Danny as her son by the Indian Chief. It is, however, not true.

As far as Heinrich Faber is concerned I have tried to find Civil War service records for him, but was unable to find any. I also searched for a grave marker and an obituary for him, but was unable to find any. The article in the book, "The History of Early Greeley County," only identifies a white settler that was captured and escaped as Henrich. It does not provide a last name, and in that story, he wasn't her husband. I don't know where the name Faber originated.

The story of an Anna is a real one. It is explained in the previous chapter. Her maiden name, however, was Brewster, not Faber. And her married name was Morgan. That was her brother's name as well and that information is confirmed on her gravestone and obituary comments as well. Anna was also captured by the Indians. Her capture was near Delphos, Kansas. She also had a son by an Indian Chief, but her son's name was Ira. (There is also a confirmed grave marker and obituary for Ira). Upon her release from the Indians, she returned to her husband, Mr. James Morgan, who never seemed to get over her having a baby by an Indian. Ira soon died. He was 17 months old. Anna was committed to an Insane Asylum and died there in 1902.

Mrs. Nadine Cheney from Greeley County also told me that, reportedly, the Coldharts refused to answer any questions after their performance at Marienthal, Georgia. Based on the above I don't believe this story is the correct story behind the legend regarding the ghost of White Woman Creek. Again, as they say, "Close, but no cigar."

10. THE NEBRASKA PLUM CREEK AND OAK CREEK MASSACRES

ABOUT THE TIME I THINK I HAVE HEARD IT ALL ABOUT THE Ghost of White Woman Creek, something comes up that makes me question what I have previously heard or read about it. This story is another "possible" version of the Ghost of White Woman Creek, even though it did not take place in or near the creek, the details are provable. Most of them anyway.

From May 1, 1865 to September 6, 1865, a Ms. Sarah Belle Raymond traveled by wagon train from Missouri to Virginia City, Montana Territory. Her exact age at the time is unknown. She was more than likely a teenager. What's unique about her trip is that she kept a dairy and recorded the events that occurred on the trip on a daily basis.[89] Years later, after Sarah had married a Mr. James Madison Herndon, some of her friends in Virginia City that knew about Sarah's dairy persuaded her to publish her dairy in a local newspaper, the "Rocky Mountain Husbandman," which she did. She did it in the early 1880's.

Almost 20 years later, an editor for the Burr Printing House offered to publish her diary in a book. The Burr Printing House published it in 1902. It's titled, "Days on the Road: Crossing the

Plains, 1865."[90] The original copy is, reportedly, in the Library of Congress. The author is Sarah Raymond Herndon. A copy of the diary can be purchased via the internet. Amazon has a few copies available and you can even read it page-by-page on the internet if so desired. It has 270 pages and is easy reading and can be read in an afternoon. I highly recommend it, especially if you are a history buff.

Not only is Sarah's book a collaboration of the events that occurred, but one can also go to "Find A Grave" on the internet and see her ancestry and grave stone.[91]

The reason I think Sarah's story should be included with the others is because it is so similar to the others it is almost scary. Yes, it could all be just a coincidence, but the odds of that happening are extremely high.

Sarah states that her wagon train, known as "the Hardinbrooke train" was near Fort Kearney, Nebraska Territory when they were confronted with evidence of the hazards of their journey. On Saturday, June 10, 1865, the train came upon a group of eleven graves. They were the graves of eleven men that were killed by Indians the previous August. There was a kind of bulletin-board near the graves stating the circumstances of their death.

Reportedly, there had been a party of fourteen people. Twelve men and two women. The women were wives of two of the men. They were camped at a place called Plum Creek, which was a short distance away from the grave site. They were all at breakfast, except for one man who had gone to the creek for water when the Indians attacked. The man at the creek hid in the brushes or there would have been none to tell of the massacre.

There had been no robberies, killings or theft committed by the Indians on this road all summer, and emigrants had become careless and traveled in small parties. This group of people did not suspect that an Indian was even near until they were surrounded and the slaughter commenced. All but one of the men were killed and scalped, and the two women were taken prisoners. The Indians took what they wanted of the provisions, burned the wagons, and ran off with the horses.

The one man that escaped had been getting water from a nearby stream when the Indians attacked. The Indians didn't see him. After the attack, he went as fast as he could to the nearest station for help. The soldiers pursued the Indians, had a fight with them, and rescued the women. One of them had seen her husband killed and scalped and was insane when rescued. She died upon arrival back at the station. It is unknown what her name is and where she was buried.

Also, reportedly, the other woman was the wife of the man that escaped. They were from St. Joe, Missouri. It is unknown what happened to them after that. However, according to an article in the "The Kearney Hub" newspaper by Lori Potter, a Hub staff writer, the other woman was Nancy Jane Morton of Sidney, Iowa. Nancy Jane Fletcher was born February 8, 1845. She was the seventh of fourteen children. Nancy became the bride of Thomas F. Morton on December 20, 1860 at the tender age of fifteen. The article states, "A wounded Nancy Morton remained a captive until Jan. 18, 1865, when she was ransomed by traders sent to the upper Powder River country of Wyoming by Maj. John Wood of the 7th Cavalry." The Kearney Hub article goes on to say that she passed the Plum Creek mass gravesite on her way to her father's home in Sidney, Iowa, after she was rescued. and that she later remarried and lived until 24 Aug 1912.[92]

A search on the Find A Grave web site indicates her parents were Samuel and Charlotte Fletcher. Nancy's first husband, Thomas Frank Morton, was killed in the Plum Creek Massacre.[93] After she was rescued she later married a George Stevens and is buried in Grand Junction, Iowa.[94] Extensive research on the massacre is present in the book, "Captive of the Cheyenne: The Story of Nancy Jane Morton & the Plum Creek Massacre" by Russ Czaplewski.[95] According to the Find A Grave web site on Nancy, this book was published by the Dawson County Museum in Lexington, Nebraska. It is also available on line through Amazon. Mrs. Morton later wrote a remarkable account of her 1864-1865 captivity.[96] Also, extensive research on this and other Indian massacres can be found in Gregory and Susan Michno's book titled "A Fate Worse Than Death."[97]

A John Fletcher was also killed in the Plum Creek Massacre. He was a cousin to Williams S. Fletcher and Nancy Jane Fletcher Morton Stevens.[98]

Sarah recorded in her diary that on Friday, June 23, 1865, that they were camping in Colorado and had come through Julesberg. She stated it was a rather insignificant looking place to have such notoriety as it has had in the newspapers. There they met with a company of soldiers with about 20 Indian prisoners. There were captured near Fort Laramie and they were taking them to Fort Kearney. The soldiers said they had a fight with about 1000 Indians three weeks earlier. There were no soldiers killed, although a number were seriously wounded, and they lost a good many horses. There were squaws and papooses with the prisoners, though they were not held captive. The soldiers said the Indians in the fight were Sioux and Cheyenne.

On page 174, Sarah says, "We came twenty miles without stopping and then camped for the night. We are near a fine spring of most excellent water—Barrel Spring it is called."

And I'm wondering if she's referring to the Barrel Springs in Greeley County, KS. And it should also be noted that the Indians the soldiers fought were Cheyenne Indians. The story of the 11 men killed and the two women captured are also all too familiar.

There is a memorial to those that lost their lives in the Plum Creek Massacre that was erected in remembrance by Phelps Co. on Nov 9, 1930. It should be noted that it states on the memorial the massacre occurred on August 7, 1864. (See Fig #1 Plum Creek Massacre Memorial). However, there is a Historical Marker at the site of the Plum Creek massacre cemetery that says the massacre occurred on August 8, 1864.[99] Whatever day it occurred is moot. It should, however, be noted that in the first part of August there was a lot of hostile Indian activity all along the Oregon Trail and routes westward.

This raid on the wagon train of freighters along the Platte River marked the start of a full-scale Indian war that burned in the Great Plains for more than a quarter century. The attack came to be known as the Plum Creek Massacre.[100][101][102][103] and would be the spark igniting what came to be known as the "Indian War of 1864."[104]

As told in numerous books/article, on August 7,1864, a suspiciously friendly party of some 20 Cheyenne Dog Soldiers and Sioux warriors dropped in for a visit at the Oak Grove Station, which was located about one and one-fourth miles southeast of Oak, Nebraska. There were some ranch workers there at the time. They, apparently, were outside the ranch house talking when the

Indians suddenly attacked and killed two ranchers and wounded two more. Eleven ranch workers ran into the ranch house and barricaded themselves inside. One worker ran into a grove of trees and escaped being harmed. The Indians then stole and destroyed about $50,000 in property and livestock. However, as an ox train began to approach, the Indians rode off. The next day, after the survivors had fled, the Indians returned, setting fire to the original buildings. The site today is commemorated with a Pony Express monument.

Also, the next day (August 8th), which is the day the Indians returned to the Oak Grove Station to burn it, there were two more Indian attacks nearby. The Indians were, in all likelihood, the same Indians that attacked the wagon train on Plum Creek. The first attack was between the Oak Grove Station and the Kiowa Ranch Station. In this attack, a war party of Indians chased a passenger filled stagecoach. No one was killed. However, on the same day just a mile and a half from there was the Bowie Ranch. At the Bowie Ranch, a couple was slain and some $10,000 worth of property and livestock were stolen and/or destroyed.

A Mr. John G. Ellenbecker of Marysville, Kansas also wrote about the Indian raids on the Little Blue River. He wrote an article titled "Oak Grove Massacre, Indian Raids on the Little Blue River in 1864,"[105] and had it published in the Marysville Advocate-Democrat. I'm not sure of what year it was published, but I'm guessing it was around 1952 since he states that the memories of the survivors were excellent considering it was 62 years after they had been released/freed by their captors. It is an excellent article about the Indian activity during the first week or so of August 1864. He spent months collecting data for the article and even corresponded with the survivors of the various massacres. This article is perhaps the most accurate and complete record of the massacres that occurred along the Little Blue River in the Kansas and Nebraska territories. His efforts and recording of the events are a valuable contribution to the frontier history. I highly recommend it.

Mr. Ellenbecker expounds on what Ms. Sarah Belle Raymond succinctly covers in her short diary of the grave site she saw near Plum Creek. He aptly covers the period leading up to the massacres, thoroughly explaining why the Indians were upset with the white man and what they were doing about it. He points out that the warfare was particularly serious on the Overland or Oregon trail, along the Little Blue and the Platte rivers, and that many cruel Indian raids were carried out, and many valiant defenses were made by the soldiers and other white people living on the plains.

He points out that there were numerous little army posts. These forts were about 40 miles apart and they were manned with about 30 men at each post and their mission was to protect the U.S. mail and travel in general along the Overland Trail. However, because there were so few soldiers, they often had to divide their resources in order to escort wagon trains and stage coaches and repair telegraph lines. It proved to be extremely difficult for them.

Also, because their forces were small and then split up because the territory they had to protect was so large, their mission was almost impossible to meet. Couple that with the fact that the American Civil War was going on and the government needed troops to fight it. Consequently, these little out-posts were never fully manned, and when they were, they were probably manned with soldiers recouping from the Civil War and were most likely not the best or brightest ones available. Never-the-less, they were able to put up a strong resistance to the Indians that were continuously harassing them by stealing their horses, mules, cattle, and anything else they could.

In Mr. Ellenbecker's article, he vividly points out who was killed, how they were killed, and where they were killed. He also clearly identifies who was taken captive and what happened to them during their captivity. His article tells of the capture by the Sioux and Cheyenne Indians of four persons, who were not ransomed for nearly a year afterwards. About 40 people were killed, among these being nine members of the Eubank families. (See Chapter XI for more information on the Eubank families)

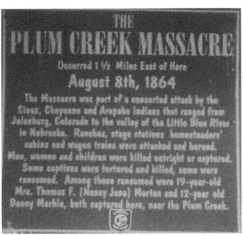

Plum Creek Massacre Memorial

11. OTHER NEBRASKA BATTLES/MASSACRES

BESIDES THE PLUM CREEK MASSACRE, THERE WERE OTHER Indian battles and massacres that occurred in Nebraska during this time-period that warrant mentioning. They are similar stories about Indian massacres involving killed and/or massacred women.

Although it was illegal for settlers to make their homes in Nebraska because the area was officially reserved for Indians, a great number of them began to homestead there. The settlers traveled on the Oregon, California, and Mormon Trails across Nebraska. This made the Plains Indians angry because it was their home, not the white man's. The whites then started to demand that Nebraska be designated a territory of the federal government in order to legalize the settlements that were already there. In 1854, the U.S. Congress passed the Kansas-Nebraska Act, which created the Territory of Nebraska and included parts of Colorado, Wyoming, Montana, and North and South Dakota. At the time, there were approximately 60,000 Plains Indians living there and a lot of them were in permanent villages along the Missouri and Platte Rivers and their tributaries.

Because the U.S. Government legalized the territory, more

and more settlers began to go there and establish homesteads and small towns. The influx of more whites taking the Indian hunting grounds and settling on what the Indians felt was theirs, led to many small conflicts between the two. For years, relations between the Cheyenne and the white man followed an ugly pattern of some settler killing a Cheyenne woman from one clan, that clan killing some settlers in revenge, and then angry soldiers killing some bewildered Cheyennes from a different clan, prompting their own kin to take revenge, and starting the cycle anew.

One of the first major clashes to take place was the Blue Water Battle which was sometimes called the Battle of Ash Hollow. It was fought in western Nebraska in 1855.

The Blue Water/Ash Hollow Battle in 1855 was an effort by the government to punish the Sioux for their depredations following the Grattan Fight near Fort Laramie, Wyoming in 1854. The Army sent out Colonel William S. Harney and an expedition of 600 men from Fort Leavenworth, Kansas to take care of the matter.

On September 3rd, 1855, Colonel Harney attacked the Sioux village called Little Thunder in Blue Water Creek Valley, which was above the creek's junction with the North Platte River. When Colonel Harney's dragoons attacked from two different directions, the Indians scattered. The dragoons, however, were able to kill 80 warriors, wounded five, and captured 70 women and children. Only four dragoons were killed and seven wounded. The rest of the Sioux and Northern Cheyenne that was in the vicinity managed to avoid the troops.

The Blue Water/Ash Hollow Battle Site is now on private property, but a 40-acre Ash Hollow State Historical Park overlooks the battlefield. It is located in Garden County on U.S. Highway 26, just west of Lewellyn, Nebraska.[106]

Because of the horrible conditions on the Cheyenne and Arapaho reservations, they began to retaliate by attacking stage coaches and settlements along the Oregon Trail. Along the upper Little Blue River in Nebraska about 100 people were killed.[107]

More skirmishes continued so the federal government sent in troops in 1859 to subdue the Indians. It was a difficult time for the federal government because the Civil War started in 1861 and the troops that were sent to quell the Indian problems out west were needed back east to fight in the Civil War. Many troops had to leave and go back east. The Indians knew this and tried to capitalize on it. The Sioux, Cheyenne, and Arapaho Indians increased their efforts to drive the white man out of their land.

Just prior to the Sand Creek Massacre, Cheyenne Dog Soldiers, Arapaho, and Sioux warriors attacked along the Overland Trail. The settlements along the Little Blue River in Nebraska were attacked in August 1864. The raids along the Little Blue River resulted in 38 settlers killed, nine wounded, and five captured.

On August 7th, 1864, the Indians attacked stage stations and ranches along the Oregon Trail. They attacked nearly every settlement for 400 miles from Julesberg, Colorado to Big Sandy, Nebraska. This led to the Battle of the Little Blue on August 17th, 1864 in which the military and local militia drove back the Indians. It did not stop them however, because many small skirmishes continued after that.

Also on August 7, 1864, near "the Narrows" which is near where the Eubanks families lived, the Indians attacked and killed and scalped several family members.[108] "The Narrows" was a troublesome portion of the Oregon Trail. It was just northwest of the town of Oak, Nebraska. It was so named because here the Oregon Trail was squeezed between the Little Blue River and a stretch of high, rugged bluffs which were almost impassable for wagons. The Trail became so tight in some areas that there was room for only one wagon at a time to pass through this "narrow" portion of the trail. It became an ideal area for the Indians to ambush an emigrant train, a freight train, or a stagecoach.

Mrs. Lucinda Eubanks,[109] her two children, (Isabella,[110] age three and William,[111] age 9 months), Miss Laura Roper,[112] age 16, and Ambrose Asher,[113] age 9, were taken prisoner and held captive for months. The warriors took their captors to the Cheyenne and Arapaho encampment on the Smoky Hill River. On August 12th, Arapaho Peace Chief Left Hand made a trade with the warriors for Ambrose Asher, Laura Roper, and Isabella Eubank. The warriors thought Isabella Eubank was Laura Roper's child. Lucinda Eubank and her baby William were sold to a renegade Sioux warrior named Two Face. Consequently, Lucinda's 3-year old child, Isabelle, stayed with Laura Roper and Peace Chief Left Hand and not with her mother, Lucinda. Arapaho Peace Chief Left Hand turned out to be a kind, decent and highly educated Indian. He treated Ambrose, Laura, and Isabelle with respect and kindness.

On September 11, 1864, Arapaho Peace Chief Left Hand, Cheyenne Chief Black Kettle, and five other Cheyenne Chiefs went to Denver to try and negotiate a truce with the Army in exchange for returning their captors. The truce was negotiated with Major Wynkoop, the commander of the First Colorado Cavalry, who had arrived there from Fort Lyon, Colorado. Ambrose, Laura and Isabelle and a young boy (12 years old) named Daniel (Danny) Marble[114] (who was captured in the Plum Creek massacre) were released on that day. It was thought that the scarcity of food and the harshness of the coming winter is what prompted them to release their captives. They, reportedly, also offered to send their warriors with the white troops to fight the Kiowas and Comanches.

Laura Roper, once released by the Indians, was reunited with her family. Isabelle Eubank was released but was never reunited with her mother. She was turned over to a Dr. Bondsall of Denver, Colorado who took care of her. Unfortunately, Isabelle never recovered from her ordeal and died shortly thereafter. Ambrose Asher was sent to live with his grandmother in Quincy, Illinois. Daniel (Danny) Marble had been taken from a wagon train near Plum Creek, Nebraska along with a Mrs. Nancy Jane Morton, who was the wife of one of the wagon train owners, T.F. Morton.[115]

Danny Marble, once released, was befriended by a Private William F. Smith of Company D, 1st Colorado Cavalry. He took Danny under his wing. The 1st Colorado Company took up a collection and collected $76.50 for Danny for clothing and other necessities. However, Danny soon caught typhoid fever and died on November 7th.[116] After her release, Laura Roper sent a letter to Ann Marble, Danny's mother, on January 7th, notifying her of Danny's death.[117]

Mrs. Eubank, would be abused and assaulted for nearly a year by the Indian called Two Face. She and William were finally brought to Fort Laramie, Wyoming in May, 1865. Two Face and another warrior named Blackfoot were tried and hanged for the abuse of Mrs. Eubank and her son, William. It wasn't until Mrs. Eubank, upon her release by Two Face, learned of her daughter's (Isabelle) death. Mrs. Eubank was said to have been "not right" after that. She did, however, make her way back east with her son. She later remarried a Doctor Franklin Atkinson in Missouri.

Fortunately, all this is documented. Laura Louise Roper died March 11th, 1930 in Enid, Oklahoma. Laura Louise Roper married a Mr. James Kinney Vance as her gravestone and obituary indicate. His obituary simply states, "He was last known to be living in Lawton, OK in 1910." His gravestone only gives a year of death. It does not provide a month and day.[118] I suspect Laura and James divorced and he never remarried. Together they had five children and were living in Oklahoma. They must have divorced because she then married a Mr. Elijah Soper and they had four more children.[119]

As for the majority of the Eubank families being massacred, it is documented on their obituaries and grave monuments (See Find A Grave Web sites on Joseph Eubank, Sr.,[120] Joseph Eubank Jr.,[121] William J. Eubank,[122] Fred Eubank,[123] Dora Eubank,[124] James Eubank,[125] Henry Eubank,[126] and William S. Fletcher (who was Nancy Fletcher (Morton) later Stevens brother.[127]

After the Eubanks massacre, most of the settlers fled east to Beatrice and Marysville or northwest to Fort Kearny on the Platte River for protection. On June 3, 1864, the post office agent at Fort Leavenworth, Kansas complained to General Curtis of westbound mail robberies by the Cheyenne. On the same date, Colorado Governor John Evans sent a second request for troops to General Curtis.

This led to the Sand Creek Massacre of November 29, 1864 (See Chapter II, Part III, Sand Creek Massacre) and other Indian Battles in the 1860's involving the Cheyenne Indians such as the Battle of Mud Springs, 4 thru 6 February, 1865, the Battle of Rush Creek, 8-9 February, 1865, and the Little Blue River Raid, 7-9 August.[128] Unfortunately, even in the 1870's, some factions of the Cheyenne were still angry and not through fighting with the white man, especially after the Indians victory over the white man in the Battle of Little Bighorn [129][130] (unofficially known as Custer's Last Stand) on 25 June, 1876 because in July of 1876 about 1,000 Cheyenne joined forces with the Sioux at Warbonnet Creek (which is in Sioux County, Nebraska) to fight the white man again.[131][132]

The Indians were attacked by elements of the 5th Cavalry. It was a brief skirmish, resulting in only one Indian killed and that was done by a scout for the Cavalry. His name was William F. "Buffalo Bill" Cody. He claimed to have taken a scalp off a warrior named "Yellow Hair", and held it up and yelled, "The first scalp for Custer!", but this was later disputed and refuted.[133]

12. CAPTIVE DEPREDATIONS & REPARATIONS

IN THE BEGINNING OF THE COUNTRY'S GROWTH, INDIANS killed and captured many of the early settlers. There were thousands of captives taken by both sides. The Indians did it and so did the white settlers. It was, and is, impossible to accurately say how many. There were no means of recording each occurrence. Indians took Spanish, Mexican, European, and American captives as well as other Indians—people of all color hues and bloodlines and the settlers did the same thing.

The very act of relating the stories of the killings, captures, etc. are replete with details of killing, mutilation, abuse, and rape. The subject has been studied by scholars for many years. Naturally, early on the main focus was on the eastern part of the country. The west (frontier) was still developing and expanding.

While there were certainly many atrocities committed by the Indians in the early part of the country's history, it was nothing compared to the number of them committed in the period from 1830 to 1885 in the mid-west, especially in the Texas area. For example, Gregory and Susan Michnos state in their book:

"Texas was particularly hard hit. in the years 1865 through the first half of 1867, thirty-five counties reported a total of 162 killed, twenty-four wounded, and forty-three captured, plus 2,430 sheep and goats, 3,781 horses and 30,838 cattle stolen. wise county reported that between 1865 and 1870 it was raided twenty-one times and had twelve citizens murdered and five captured."

"one estimate is that about 400 people were captured within 100 miles of parker county, Texas. jack CounTy reported 200 citizens killed and captured between 1859 and 1871. montague county lost fortY-three citizens killed or captured in 1866 alone. in other Texas counties between 1873 and 1875 there were forty-five killed, fifteen wounded, and two captured. a compilation showing depredations from 1865 to 1879 shows 407 texans killed by Indians, seventy-six wounded, and eighty-one women and children carried off, plus 20,521 horses and mules, and 43,392 cattle stolen. the report also stated that seventy-seven Indians were killed, twenty-nine wounded and three captured, along with the recovery of 6,871 horses and cattle."[134]

Additionally, the Michnos book states:

"the possibility of becoming an Indian captive on the frontier was very real, and although a western overland trip could be hazardous, the stay-at-home frontier settlers faced dangers many times worse. there are no comprehensive statistics available to accurately total up the number OF captives taken during the american western movement. below, however,

are some various estimations that give a hint of the problem's enormity."

"prior to the period of our study, from 1540 to 1820, estimates range from 5,000 to 10,000 people captured by Indians along the Texas-Sonora border. Durango alone lost 1,446 women and children as prisoners to the Indians between 1822 and 1855. The Kiowas estimated that from 5 to 7 percent of their population were captives. In 1821, the Comanches held 900 prisoners, but by 1855, they held 2,000. Probably about 1,000 Americans were taken captive between 1860 and 1875."

"The official count of casualties in the 1862 Minnesota Uprising was established at 644 dead, plus about 300 captives. In Kansas and Nebraska there were about 400 citizens murdered in 1866 and 1867. In Nebraska, fifty-two were killed, wounded, or captured in just ten days in August 1864. In Kansas in 1867-1868 the State Legislature visited five counties: Ellsworth, Saline, Ottawa, Cloud, and Mitchell, and took 120 depredation claims totaling almost $59,000. War Department statistics for Kansas in 1868-1869 showed 158 people murdered, sixteen wounded, forty-eight scalped, fourteen women "outraged," one man, four women, and seven children captured. There were far more noncombatants killed in the Indian Wars than in the Civil War."[135]

We all have in our minds images of the Indian plight. According to Gregory and Susan Michno in their book, "A Fate Worse Than Death," there has been a dramatic shift in perception about old heroes and villains. At first the Indians were the bad guys, however, "today white Americans are depicted as savage and greedy barbarians, while the Indians are said to have lived in peace with ecological wisdom. These role reversals illuminate history less than they simply elevate one group at the expense of another."[136]

At first blush, the Indian is thought of as being the victim because the white man was encroaching on his territory, killing all the buffalo and other game, and generally forcing the Indian out of their ancestral territory and either move or be killed.

Glenda Riley wrote a book titled "The Female Frontier" in which she describes how she believes the Indians treated their captives. She says that not all the captive's experiences were negative, that some formed bonds of affection and often wanted to stay with their captors. [137] However, according to Gregory and Susan Michno, this is hogwash. In their book, they state that Riley didn't believe a lot of the survivor statements and that her research was inadequate. [138]

According to the Michnos, almost all the captives taken by the Indians were treated horribly and did not want to stay with the Indians. Yes, there were some that stayed, even when offered a chance to return to their families. It generally occurred when the captives taken were very young, had been with the Indians a long time, and in a lot of cases could not even remember their family. They were forced to survive, and after so much time with the Indians they assimilated into the tribe. They were "brainwashed" or as some would say they had what would later become known as the "Stockholm Syndrome," which could be found in some survivors because they would "parrot" much of what they learned during their captivity.

A case in point is Cynthia Ann Parker. She is perhaps the most famous and celebrated of all the Indian captives. Cynthia was kidnapped/captured on May 19, 1836 at an early age (possibly 8 years old, her birth year is unknown) by a Comanche war band which had massacred her family's settlement. She lived with the Comanche for 24 years, completely forgetting her white ways.[139] A Comanche family adopted her. She married a Comanche chief and they had three children.

In December 1860, some Texas Rangers spotted a small band of Comanche that was rumored to have captives. The Rangers attacked. It is known as "The Battle of Pease River." During the attack a Ranger spotted an Indian squaw carrying a child fleeing from the Rangers and the battle area. She was caught by one of the Rangers and he probably would have killed her but he heard her yell, "Americano, Americano" so he held his fire. It was then learned that the Rangers had possibly "rescued" Cynthia Ann Parker. She was then approximately 34 years old. She no longer spoke English. She was completely assimilated into the Comanche culture. She thought of herself as Comanche. It wasn't until she heard her uncle, Colonel Isaac Parker, who met up with her days later, mention his niece's name (Cynthia Parker) that they knew for sure it was Cynthia Parker because she slapped her chest and said, "Me Cincee Ann."[140]

Cynthia Ann Parker returned to her birth family. She captured the country's imagination. Tens of thousands of Texas families, and many more throughout the country, had suffered the loss of family members, especially children, in Indian raids. Plus, she was the granddaughter of a famous American patriot who had met a violent end in far-off Texas.

Cynthia had a hard time adjusting to her new life. Although she had her daughter (the child she was carrying when rescued), Cynthia missed her sons and the Comanche life. She was very unhappy. In 1864, her daughter, Topusana, caught influenza and died of pneumonia. Cynthia went downhill from there. She began refusing food and water and resisted encouragement to save herself. She died in 1871. Her son, Quannah Parker, moved her body to Post Oak Mission Cemetery near Cache, Oklahoma. When he died in 1911 he was buried next to her. Their bodies were moved in 1957 to the Fort Sill Post Cemetery at Fort Sill, Oklahoma. (See Historical Marker)

Cynthia Ann Parker . Photo courtesy of
"DeGolyer Library, Southern Methodist University,
Lawrence T. Jone III Texas Photographs"

Texas Historical Survey Committee Memorial of Cynthia Ann Parker

Cynthia Ann Parker's Gravestone

Unlike Cynthia, many tried to escape their captivity, however, they were almost always recaptured shortly afterwards and treated even more harshly. Their family members were killed, scalped, mutilated, burned alive, shot with arrows and lances in front of the captive. The captives were most often taken to an Indian camp and treated as slaves. They were barely fed and beaten almost constantly. Often times it was the Indian women who treated the captives the worse, especially female captives. In most cases the white women captives were, in addition to being beaten, starved, and treated as slaves, they were raped repeatedly and many times gang raped by the warriors. It was, in most cases, horrendous, and as the Michnos say it was "a fate worse than death."

Glenda Riley in her book says that using statistics of captives taken in New England between 1675 and 1763, about 62 percent of the captives were male and 52 percent were adults. She posits that data collected for the trans-Mississippi West would show a similar pattern, however, it does not, according to the Michnos. In the West, only 35 percent of the captives were male and only 25 percent were adults. There is a strikingly different capture pattern that does not appear to be caused by luck-of-the-draw.

In the West there were hundreds, perhaps thousands of white captives. Almost all of them had bad experiences. As mentioned above, there were more females and children taken captive than men. There were many reasons for this.

The total damage that the Indians did to the early settlers was huge. Unfortunately, there was, and is, no way to determine the exact amount of property lost and lives taken due to there being no accurate record of the events. It is for the most part a best guess. It is, however, undeniable that the Indians destroyed thousands of homesteads, stole thousands of horses, and killed and/or captured thousands of settlers. The Indians say the same thing happened to them.

In the book, "A Fate Worse Than Death," by the Michnos it states,

> "In 1796, the U.s. Congress passed a law to provide compensation to both Indians and whites for depredations committed upon each other. Claims were filed and adjudicated as late as 1920. Poor record keeping and lost files make it impossible to determine exactly how many claims whites filed because of losses due to Indian depredations. They numbered in the thousands up to 1891, when all remaining cases were sent from Congress to the Court to settle. From 1891 to 1920, the Court tried 10,841 cases, and paid less than 13 percent of the damages claimed. From 1796 to 1890, only three percent of the claims were paid. Untold thousands of white settlers lost lives and property due to Indian raids. Life and limb were not remunerated—only property—but even so, pitiably few were compensated."[141]

So, in effect, there was a law to compensate both white and Indian since 1796. Both sides knew it and it apparently helped spawn the killing and capturing of whites by the Indians. They knew they could get "ransom" money/food/guns/ammo/clothing from the U.S. Army for the prisoners they had captured. Plus, they could use their captors as slaves until they were compensated for them by the Army. It was a win-win for them. And it just generated more and more violence on the frontier. It wasn't until years later that the Indian tribes submitted documentation to Congress for their losses. In the meantime, the Army and the ransom system was their way of getting paid.

It caused problems for the whites because in most cases the entire family was killed except for the young children or females. There were exceptions, of course, but how can a family request reimbursement for their losses when the entire family is killed. It was left to the surviving relatives to request it. And that took months and months. And then the government red tape came into it. Most requests for reimbursement were denied due to improper reimbursement documentation. It was sent back to be redone and correctly resubmitted. One of the problems was the family wanted to be reimbursed for the loss of a family member but the law only allowed reimbursement for property—not life. Then came the problem of accurately documenting the correct value of the property. If it was questioned by Congress, it was again sent back to the originator. And it seemed to be ALMOST ALWAYS questioned. Consequently, there were few reimbursements to the settlers or their relatives.

One must remember that the process of getting paperwork back and forth to Congress in those days was a slow and tedious project. Especially when you consider that most surviving victims were illiterate and lived in areas where there was no one to help them write or prepare the correct paperwork. In some cases, the process took so long that the surviving captor had lived out the remainder of his/her life before the reimbursement was approved by Congress.

The Kiowa Indians under Chief Satanta captured Mrs. Mary Box and her three children in Texas on 15 August 1866, Satanta released them to a Captain Sheridan in the U.S. Army at Fort Dodge in September for around $2,800 in supplies and money. When General William T. Sherman, on an inspection tour, arrived at Fort Dodge shortly after the affair, he instructed Captain Sheridan not to purchase any other captives from the Indians. When Indian Agent I. C. Taylor learned of Captain Sheridan's ransom payment, he became angry and wrote the Commissioner of Indian Affairs, D. N. Cooley, on September 30th and wanted to know under whose authority Sheridan was allowed to pay the Indians. He reminded the Commissioner that every prisoner purchased from the Indians amounts to the same as granting them a license to go and commit the same overt act. The Indians believed that stealing white women was more of a lucrative business than stealing horses.[142]

Apparently, the U.S. Government and the U.S. Army no longer wanted to make ransom payments about this time. And this dramatically reduced, and in some areas, completely stopped the killing and taking of hostages to ransom them. The Indians realized that it wasn't going to get them anywhere.

13. CONCLUSIONS

THERE ARE MANY GREAT ARTICLES, STORIES, BOOKS AND pamphlets written about the legend of White Woman Creek. Which one is true? We may never know for sure. Time and the lack of documentation have clouded the legend. Perhaps it is better that way. At this point in time we can only imagine what the real story behind the naming of the creek is.

As far as I'm concerned, the most believable and credible story is the one written by Grace Bjork, wife of Harold Bjork, that was written and later compiled by Mildren Waldren and published in the Greeley County Republican (See Bibliography #60) about the white woman that was massacred at Barrel Springs on July 4, 1888. It fits. No one knows her name. There is no grave marker and flowers have grown in the area where she was buried. It makes a sweet story and she also died on the 4th of July, our country's Independence Day!

As for her ghost still roaming the White Woman Creek. It still may be. I hope that she has since found peace and no longer roams the creek bed moaning for her lost husband/family.

I only know that she got my attention and that I, for sure, will not be going back, partly because of time/distance, plus I don't need to have the hair on the back of my neck raised so high ever again because of a ghost. I do hope that she has found peace and stopped her wailing.

BIBLIOGRAPHY

Notes: Introduction

1. Legends of America, "American History-The Mighty Missouri River," p. 2, http://www.legendsofamerica.com/mo-missouririver.html.
2. Ibid., p. 2.
3. Journal of Onomastics, Vol. 47, 1999, Issue 3, written by Donald M. Lance, pp., 281-290, http://dx.doi.org/10.1179/nam.1999.47.3.281.
4. Question and Answer Article, Atlanta Journal-Constitution, dated 7 Feb 2017.
5. Kansas Historical Society, "Ghost Stories," pp. 1-2. https://www.kshs.orgkansapedia/ghost-stories/12066.

Notes: Chapter 1

6. Cheyenne Tribe (Access Genealogy), pp 1-15. http://www.access-genealogy.com/native/cheyenne-tribe.htm
7. Cheyenne Indians, p.1. www.indians.org/articlescheyenne-indians.html
8. Teepees from Nomadics, "Native American Facts For Kids, Cheyenne Tribe," pp. 2-7. http://www.bigorrin.org/cheyenne_kids.htm.

9. Article in the Greeley County Republican, Horace Greeley Museum Chatter Section, dated, Wednesday, January 29, 2014, written by Mildred Waldren, p.10.

10. Article "WHAT is an AMERICAN INDIAN HORSE?", http://www.Indianhorse.com/old/define.htm, pp. 1-2.

11. Horse Preview Magazine, "The Plains Indians Bridle", pp. 1-3, posted 03/07/2001, http://www.horse-previews.com/0301articles/plainsindianbridle.html.

12. Article by Pamela Gifford, eHow Contributor, "About the Cheyenne Indians", pp. 1-5, http://www.ehow.com/about_4568838_cheyenne-indians.html.

Notes: Chapter 2 Part 1

13. Brian Kilmeade and Don Yaeger, "Andrew Jackson and The Miracle of New Orleans," Prologue, pp. 2–3.

14. Ibid.,p. 7.

15. Ibid., p. 7.

16. Ibid., p. 6.

17. Ibid., p. 15.

18. Ibid., p. 10.

19. Ibid., p. 33. (letter from Andrew Jackson to his wife, Rachel).

20. Ibid., p. 35 and Crockett,, "Narrative of the Life of David Crockett," 1834, p., 92.

21. Brian Kilmeade and Don Yaeger, "Andrew Jackson and The Miracle of New Orleans," pp. 41-47.

22. Encyclopedia of Alabama, "Battle of Horseshoe Bend," by Ove Jensen (Horseshoe Bend National Military Park), pp. 1-3.

23. Military History, "Battle of Horseshoe Bend (4th)," edited by Jennifer Van Overdam, http://militaryhistory.about.com/od/warof1812/p/battle-of-horseshoe-bend.htm.

24. "The Battle of Lake Erie," National Park Service, page 2., (/pevi/historyculture/battle_le_p2.htm)

25. War of 1812: Big Night in Baltimore by Hugh Howard, dated 1/6/2012k (http://www.historynet.com/war-of-1812-big-night-in-baltimore.htm)

26. North Dakota Studies, Laws and Treaties, Atkinson and O'Fallon Trade and Intercourse Treaty of 1825, page 1.

27. Manuscript, Treaty of Prairie du Chien, 1825, http://www.wisconsinhistory.org/turningpoints/search.asp?id=1620.

28. Article by Gracie bonds Staples, "Roswell honors Cherokee Nation", Living Section, Atlanta Journal-Constitution dated Saturday 9 August 2014, p., D1.gustaples@ajc.com, p. 1.

29. Article from American History Magazine, "Andrew Jackson and the Indian Removal Act," by Robert V. Remini, pp. 2-9., http://www.historynet.com/indian-removal-act.

30. Article by Mildred Waldred, Greeley County Republican, titled "Horace Greeley—Museum Chatter," Wednesday, November 19, 2014, p. 8.

31. Article by Cecile Shepherd, "Access to Greeley County Homestead Documents", Greeley County Republican, Section: Your History . Your Heritage, Wednesday, December 21, 2016, p., 10.

32. Alaska Public Lands Information Centers, "Homesteading & The Homestead Act in Alaska, pp., 1-4.https://www.alaskacenters.gov/homestead.cfm

33. American Forts—West, "Colorado," complied by Phil and Pete

Payette, last update 4 February 2015, pp. 1-11, https://www. northamericanforts.com/West/co.html.

34. Kansas Historical Society, Kansapedia, "Battle of Black Jack," pp. 1-2., https://www.kshs.org/kansapedia/battle-of-black-jack/18315.

35. Harpers Ferry National Historical Park, U.S. National Park Service, "Stories," https://www.nps.gov/hafe/learn/historyculture/stories. htm.

36. Legends of America, Buffalo Hunters in the Old West, pp. 1-3 http://www.legendsofamerica.com/we-buffalohunters.html

37. Early Ford County, "Charles Rath, Buffalo Hunter," by Ida Ellen Rath, Dodge City, KS, pp. 1-3. Kansas History Web Sites http:// www.kansashistory.us/charlesrath.html

38. Article in the Greeley County Republican, Horace Greeley, Museum Chatter Section, researched and complied by Mildred Waldren, dated Wednesday, March 27, 2013, p. 10.

Notes: Chapter 2 Part 2

39. The Civil War News & Views Open Discussion Forum, Article by David Upton, 11/2/2009, "The Battle of Solomon River," p. 1.

40. Solomon Valley Highway 24 Heritage Alliance, "The Battle of Solomon Fork, 1857, pp. 1- 5. www.hwy24.org.

Notes: Chapter 2 Part 3

41. Kansas Historical Society, "E. W. Wynkoop and the Bluff Creek

Council 1886," written by Timothy A. Zwink, Summer 1977 (Vol. 43, No. 2), pp., 217-239.

42. encyclopedia.com, "Sand Creek Massacre 1864", pp. 1-2. http://www.encyclopedia.com/topic/Sand_Creek_Massacre_1864.aspx.

43. Legends of American, "The Sand Creek Massacre", pp. 1-3. http://www.legendsofamerica.com/na-sandcreek.html.

44. Source Unknown, "The Cheyenne Indian Massacre, Exposition of the Sandy Creek Affair," Chicago Tribune, Chicago, Illinois, Tuesday, 25 July, 1865, p. 3.

45. Article, "Weekend Activities Draw Crowds to Sandy Creek Massacre National Parks", Greeley County Republican, Wednesday, December 17, 2014., p.11.

46. Article, "Sand Creek Offers Special Walking Tours", Greeley County Republican, Wednesday, September 3, 2014, p. 9.

Notes: Chapter 2 Part 4

47. Article by Jennifer Mishra, "Fort Wicked," Sunday, January 23, 2011, pp. 1-3, http://ftmorgancolorado.blogspot.com/2011/01/fort-wicked.html.

48. Article in the Reporter-Herald by Kenneth Jessen, "Fort Wicked outlasted an Indian attack," posted 09/21/2014, http://www.reporterherald.com.

49. Deadwood Magazine, Black Hills, South Dakota, "Charles Windolph was last Little Big Horn survivor," no date or page number available.

50. RoadsideAmerican.com, "Comanche, Little Bighorn Survivor", p. 1.

51. Article from University of Kansas Museum of Natural History,

"Comanche, Survivor of the Battle of the Little Bighorn," contributed by afgustaf.

Notes: Chapter 3

52. Tribal Directory, "Native American Spears," TribalDirectory.com.

53. The Saturday Evening Post, September/October 2015, Article by Todd Willinson, "A Modern Master of Western Art," pp. 42-50.

54. Swoyer's Fine Art & Collectibles, Gallery Index of Howard Terpning, http://swoyersart.com/howard_terpning/files/terpning.htm.

55. Pamphlet titled, "And Greeley County Began", written by Margaret L. Pile, Printed by the Greeley County Republican, December 1969, p. 11.

56. Article in the Greeley County Republican, "Horace Greeley Museum Chatter," dated Wednesday, February 19, 2014, written my Mildred Waldren, p. 10.

57. Article in the Greeley County Republican, "Horace Greeley Museum Chatter," dated Wednesday, August 28, 2013, written by Mildren Waldren, p. 8.

58. History of Early Greeley County, Vol. 1, "Tracks, Trails, and Tribulations," articles Ft. Wallace-Ft. Lyons Trail, and Barrel Springs Northwest, by Mrs. Grace Hougland Bjork, May, 1937, pp. 93-96.

59. History of Early Greeley County, Vol. 1, "Tracks, Trails, and Tribulations," article by Mrs. Nadine Cheney, page 92.

60. Article in the Greeley County Republican, Horace Greeley, "Museum Chatter," dated Wednesday, August 21, 2013, originally written by Grace Bjork and rewritten for publication by Mildred Waldren, p. 8.

61. Article in the Greeley County Republican, Horace Greeley Museum Section, "Your History . Your Heritage," Wednesday, June 29, 2016, researched and written by Nadine Cheney, p. 8.

62. EyeWitness to History, "Crossing the Plains, 1865," www.eyewitnesstohistory.com/plains.htm. (1999), pp. 1-6.

63. Article in the Greeley County Republican, Horace Greeley Museum Section, "Your History . Your Heritage," June 25, 2018, p.10.

64. Article in the Greeley County Republican, Horace Greeley Museum Section, "Your History . Your Heritage," October 11, 2017, compiled by Sharon Steele and Cecile Shepherd, p. 10.

Notes: Chapter 4

65. uglybridges.com, http://uglybridges.com/1183091, p. 4.

66. Article in the Greeley County Republican, dated Wednesday, June 28, 2017, Section Horace Greeley Museum, Your History . Your Heritage, "Gleaning from the Greeley County Republican," originally written by J.L. Pyles, and W.M. Glenn 8 April, 1915, p. 8.

67. Article in the Greeley County Republican, dated Wednesday, March 2, 2016, Section Horace Greeley Museum, Your History . Your Heritage, written by Nadine Chaney, p. 8.

Notes: Chapter 6

68. Article in Kansas Historical Society, "Greeley County Kansas," dated 7/29/16, unknown author, pp. 1-2. https://www..kshs.org/kansapedia/greeley-county-kansas/15291.

69. History of Early Greeley County, Vol. 1, Tracks, Trails, and Tribulations, compiled and edited by Kathy Weiser.

70. Legends of Kansas, History, Tales, and Destinations in the Land of Ahs, "The Ghost of White Woman Creek", http://www.legendsofkansas.com/ghostwhitewomancreek.html.

71. Ibid., p. 2.

72. Historical Sites (http://www.lasr.net/trave/KS+tribune+historical-soites&TraveTo=DS100702), pp. 1-3.

73. The Greenwood Encyclopedia of American Cultures, printed by the Greenwood Press in 1984, article titled "Folklore" by Amanda Rees, pp. 201-237.

74. WPA Guide to Kansas, #34 The Sunflower State, article in the chapter titled "Folklore", unknown author or print date.

75. Greeley County Republican newspaper, dated 29 June 2016, Horace Greeley Museum, article written and researched by Nadine Cheney, p. 8.

76. Article in "Seeks Ghosts" web site titled "The Ghost of White Woman Creek," dated Sunday, February 10, 2013, pp. 1-6, https://seeksghosts.blogspot.com/2013/02/the-ghost-of-white-woman-creek.html.

Note: Chapter 7

77. A rottentomatoes.com. film review, Stolen Women, Captured Hearts. https://www.rottentomatoes.com/m/black_panther_2018

Notes: Chapter 8

78. "A Fate Worse Than Death," by Gregory and Susan Michno, p. 321.

79. Delphos Kansas —"Pride of the Solomon Valley", articles by Clayton L. Hogg, Chagrin Falls, OH, pp. 1-8. http://www.chancy.org/family/Familyinfo/Kansas/delphos.html.

80. "A Fate Worse Than Death," by Gregory and Susan Michno, p. 323.

81. Find a Grave web site, "James Simeon Morgan" date of birth Dec. 1839, date of death Aug., 1904, Delta County, Colorado.

82. Find A Grave web site, "Amanda Belle "Anne" Brewster Morgan,", date of birth Dec. 12, 1844, date of death, Jul., 13, 1902, Shawnee County, Kansas, pp. 1-2

83. Ibid., p. 1.

84. Find A Grave web site, "Ira Arthur Morgan," date of birth, Dec. 3, 1869, date of death, Apr. 30, 1871, Ottawa County, Kansas, pp. 1-2.

Notes: Chapter 9

85. "The Coldharts" web site, "The Legend of White Woman Creek," created in 2012, dated 7/25/16, pp. 1-2. https://www.facebook.comTheLegendOgfWhiteWomanCreek/info/?entry_point=page_nav_about_item&tab=page_info.

86. "The Coldharts" web site, The Legend of White Woman Creek by The Coldharts, dated 8/4/16, pp. 1-6 https://thecoldharts.bandcamp.com/releases.

87. "The Coldharts" web site, The Legend of White Woman Creek, Edgar Allan 2016 Tour Dates, dated 7/24/16, pp. 1-4. http://www.thecoldharts.com/#!press/c1s5p.

88. "A Fate Worse Than Death," by Gregory and Susan Michno, p. 139.

Notes: Chapter 10

89. EyeWitness to History, "Crossing the Plains, 1865," www.eyewitnesstohistory.com/plains.htm. (1999), pp. 1-6.

90. Days on the Road: Crossing the Plains in 1865, by Sarah Raymond Herndon, dated 1902, pp. 1-278. https://archive.org/details/daysonroadcrossi01hern.

91. Find A Grave web site, "Sarah Belle Raymond Herndon, date of birth 7 Sep 1840, date of death 20 Mar 1914, p.1

92. Kearney Hub Newspaper, article by Lori Potter, a Hub staff writer, dated August 30, 2014, http://www.kearneyub.com/news/local/plum-creek-attack-unfolds-to-horror-of-soldiers, pp.1-3.

93. Find A Grave web site, "Thomas Frank Morton," date of birth 1813, date of death 8 Aug 1864, p. 1.

94. Find A Grave web site, "Nancy Jane Fletcher Stevens," date of birth 8 Feb, 1845, date of death 24 Aug, 1912, and she is buried in Grand Junction, Greene County, Iowa.

95. "Captive of the Cheyenne" by Russ Czapelwski

96. Find A Grave web site, "Nancy Jane Fletcher Stevens," date of birth 8 Feb, 1845, date of death 24 Aug, 1912, and she is buried in Grand Junction, Greene County, Iowa.

97. "A Fate Worse Than Death," by Gregory and Susan Michno, published by Caxton Press.

98. Find A Grave web site, "John Fletcher," date of birth unknown, date of death Aug 8, 1864, p. 1.

99. Legends of American, "Pony Express Stations-Page 4," unknown date, pp., 1-7. http://www.legendsofamerica.com/we-ponyexpressstations4.html.

100. Article by David Hendee, a World-Herald staff writer, "Plum Creek: A massacre that started a war," dated Aug 10, 2014, pp., 1-5. http://www.omaha.com/news/nebraska/plum-creek-a-massacre-that-started-a-war/article_e5afe5bd-08c2-5465-80a8-8c4947af43d3.html.

101. Article from Encyclopedia of Indian Wars, "Plum Creek Massacre," by Gregory F. Michno, pp. 1-2. http://www.forttours.com/pages/plumcreekneb.asp.

102. Article in the Kearney Hub, "1864 Plum Creek attack unfolds to horror of soldiers,", by Lori Potter Hub Staff Writer, dated August 30, 2014, pp. 1-3, http://www.kearneyhub.com/news/localplum-creek-attack-unfolds-to-horror-of-soldiers/article_1c037340-3008-11e4-aa70-001a4bcf887a.html.

103. Article from Lexington-Herald, Lexington, NE., "The Plum Creek Massacre and the Plum Creek Cemetery," by Danny Gruber, dated June 29, 2011, pp. 1-4.http://exch.com/news/local/the-plum-creek-cemetery/article_92067f8f-1307-5824-86dd-0b9f9f4f9b63.html. .

104. Captive of the Cheyenne by Russ Czaplewski, published by the Dawson County Historical Society, Chapter 1, p.1.

105. "Oak Grove Massacre, Indian Raids On the Little Blue River in 1864", article written by John G. Ellenbecker, Marysville, Kansas, as Printed in the Marysville Advocate-Democrat, pp. 1-30. http://freepages.genealogy.rootsweb.ancestry.com/-wynkoop/webdocs/oakgrove.htm.

Notes: Chapter 11

106. Legends of American, " Nebraska Legends-Indian War Battles & Massacres", undated, pp. 1-5. http://www.legendsofamerica.com/ ne-indianbattles.html.

107. Ibid., p. 4.

108. Ibid., p. 4.

109. Find A Grave web site, "Lucinda Walton Atkinson," date of birth 11 Aug. 1840, date of death, 4 Mar, 1913, p. 1.

110. Find A Grave web site, "Isabella Eubank," date of birth 1861, date of death 18 Feb 1865, p. 1.

111. Find A Grave web site, "William Joseph Eubank," date of birth 1 Oct. 1863, date of death 3 Mar., 1935, pp. 1-2.

112. Find A Grave web site, "Laura Louise Roper Vance,", date of birth July 16, 1848, date of death Mar. 11, 1930, pp. 1-2.

113. Find A Grave web site, "Ambrose Asher,", date of birth 1857 date of death 6 Oct, 1894, pp. 1-2.

114. Find A Grave web site, "Danny Marble," date of birth 1855, date of death 9 November 1864, Denver, Co., p. 1.

115. Find A Grave web site, "Nancy Jane Fletcher Stevens," date of birth 8Feb 1845, date of death 24 Aug 1912, p. 1.

116. "A Fate Worse Than Death" by Gregory and Susan Michno, pp. 137-139.

117. Letter to Danny's mother, Ann Marble from Laura Roper, Jan 7th, 1865.

118. Fine A Grave web site, "James Kinney Vance," date of birth Feb.,1848, date of death 1911 in Skiatook, Osage County,m Oklahoma.

119. Find A Grave web site, "Elijah Soper," date of birth 20 Mar 1843, date of death 10 Apr 1915.

120. Find A Grave web site, "Joseph Eubank, Sr.," date of birth 1802, date of death 7 Aug 1864.

121. Find A Grave web site, "Joseph Eubank, Jr.," date of birth 1835, date of death 7 Aug 1864.

122. Find A Grave web site, "William J. Eubank," date of birth 13 Oct 1838, date of death 7 Aug 1864.

123. Find A Grave web site, "Fred Eubank," date of birth 1845, date of death 7 Aug 1864.

124. Find A Grave web site, "Dora Eubank," date of birth 1850, date of death 7 Aug 1864.

125. Find A Grave web site, "James Eubank," date of birth 1851, date of death 7 Aug 1864.

126. Find A Grave web site, "Henry Eubank," date of birth 1852, date of death 7 Aug 1864.

127. Find A Grave web sit, "William S. Fletcher," date of birth 1842, date of death Aug 8, 1864.

128. Legends of America, "Nebraska Indian Battles & Massacres — Page 3", undated, pp. 3-4. http://www.legendsofamerica.com/ne-indian-battles3.html.

129. Article in the Smithsonian Magazine, "How the Battle of the Little Bighorn Was Won", by Thomas Powers, November 2010.

130. EyeWitness to history.com, "The Battle of the Little Bighorn, 1876.

131. Legends of America, "Battle at Warbonnet Creek, Nebraska", undated, p.1.

132. Liam's Web Site, "The Battle At Warbonnet Creek 1876-1877", undated, pp. 1-2.

133. Article in True West Magazine, "Buffalo Bill's First Scalp for Custer," by Paul L. Hedren, dated July 1, 2001, https://Truewestmagazine.com/author/Paul-l-Hedren/.

Notes: Chapter 12

134. "A Fate Worse Than Death," by Gregory and Susan Michno, Conclusion, pp. 471-472.

135. Ibid, Conclusion, p. 470.

136. Ibid, Introduction, p. xiii.

137. "The Female Frontier," by Glenda Riley.

138. "A Fate Worse Than Death," by Gregory and Susan Michno, Conclusion, pp. 457- 479.

139. "PARKER, CYNTHIA ANN", (https://tshaonline.org/handbllik/online/article/fpa18). tshaonline.org. Texas State Historical Society.

140. "A Fate Worse Than Death,", by Gregory and Susan Michno, Chapter 1, p. 38.

141. Ibid, Conclusion, p. 477.

142. Ibid, Chapter 8, pp. 352—355.

WIKIPEDIA ARTICLES

1. Wikipedia, "Santa Fe Trail," pp. 1-9 http://en.wikipedia.org/wiki/Santa_Fe_Trail

2. Wikipedia, "Preemption Act of 1841," pp. 1-2 http://en.wikipedia.org/wiki/Preemtion_Act_of_1841

3. Wikipedia, "Indian Removal Act," pp. 1-6 http://en.wikipedia.org/wiki/indian_Removal_Act

4. American History, pp. 2-9 http://www.historyet.com/indian-removal-act

5. Wikipedia, "Cheyenne People," pp. 1-20. http://en.wikipedia.org/wiki/Cheyenne_People.

6. Wikipedia, "Cheyenne," page last edited on 30 September 2017, https://en.wikipedia.org/w/index.php?title=Cheyenne&oldid=803118932"..

7. Wikipedia, "Go West, Young Man," pp. 1-2. http://en.wikipedia.org/wiki/Go_West,_young_man

8. Wikipedia, "California Gold Rush," pp. 1-21 http://en.wikipedia.org/wiki/California_Gold_Rush

9. Wikipedia, "Homestead Acts," pp. 1-8. http://en.wikipedia.org/wiki/Homestead_Act

10. Wikipedia, "Chisholm Trail," pp. 1-5 http://en.wikipedia.org/wiki/Chisholm_Trail

11. Wikipedia, "War of 1812," pp.1-45 http://en.wikipedia.org/wiki/War_of_1812

12. Wikipedia, "Bent's Old Fort National Historic Site," pp. 1-6 http://en.wikipedia.org/wiki/Bent%27s_Fort.

13. Wikipedia, "!st Cavalry Regiment (1885)," pp. 1-3 http://en.wikipedia.org/wiki/1st_Cavalry_Regiment_(1885)

14. Wikipedia, "Stolen Women: Captured Hearts", pp. 1-3, https://en.wikipedia.org/wiki/Stolen_Women:_Captured_Hearts.

15. Wikipedia, "Rodney A. Grant," pp. 1-2, https://en.wikipedia.org/wikiRodney_A._Grant.

16. Wikipedia, "Ted Shackelford," pp1-3, https://en.wikipedia.org/wiki/Ted_Shackelford.

17. Wikipedia, "Michael Greyeyes,", pp 1-5, https://en.wikipedia.org/wikiMichael_Greyeyes.

18. Wikipedia, "Apesanahkwat," pp 1-2, https://en.wikipedia.org/wiki/Apesanahkwat.

19. Wikipedia, "Fort Hays," pp. 1-6, https://en.wikipedia.org/wiki/Fort_Hays.

19. Kansapedia, "Battle of Black Jack," pp. 1-2., https://www.kshs.org/kansapedia/battle-of-black-jack/18315.

20. Wikipedia, "The Battle of Osawatomie," pp. 1-4., https://en.wikipedia.org/wiki/Battle_of_Osawatomie.

21. Wikipedia, "Battle of Horseshoe Bend (1814)," pp. 1-6, https://en-wikipedia.org/wiki/Battle_of_Horseshoe_Bend_%281814%29.

22. Wikipedia, "Tecumseh," pp. 1-15, https://en.wikipedia.orrg/wiki/Tecumseh.

23. Wikipedia, "The Cheyenne Language and the Cheyenne Indian Tribe," pp. 2-5, http://www.native-languages.org/cheyenne.htm.

24. Wikipedia, "Wichita, Kansas," pp. 1-2.

25. Wikipedia, "Cynthia Ann Parker."

About the Author

MR. PETERSON IS 76 YEARS OLD. HE IS A NEWCOMER TO THE writing world. He was born and raised in Tribune, KS, which is where the "White Woman Creek" in this story is located. In 1966 he joined the U.S. Army and soon graduated from the Infantry Officer Candidate School (OCS) in Fort Benning, GA. In 1968-69 he served in Vietnam as an Infantry Platoon Leader and a helicopter pilot. He was assigned to Alpha Troop, 1/9th Air Calvary Squadron, 1st Cavalry Division. He retired in 1986 as a Major. After his military service he became a police officer in the Dekalb County Police

Department, Dekalb County, GA. He retired as a Sergeant after 22 1/2 years service. Mr. Peterson married his high school sweetheart, Sandra Curtis, who also is from Tribune, KS. They have three grown sons and currently live in Grayson, Georgia.

CPSIA information can be obtained
at www.ICGtesting.com
Printed in the USA
BVHW081736010719
552377BV00013B/1316/P